Dartmoor's
Early Historic &
Medieval Remains

Dartmoor's Early Historic & Medieval Remains

by
William Crossing

QUAY
PUBLICATIONS
(BRIXHAM)

ISBN 1 870083 15 6

Published by Quay Publications (Brixham),
P.O. Box 16, Brixham, Devon TQ5 8LW

Typeset by AJL Typesetting, Paignton, Devon.
Telephone: (0803) 526103

Printed in Great Britain by Penwell Ltd.,
Parkwood, Callington, Cornwall

The photographs for chapters 2, 3, 4, 5, 6, 7, 9, 10, 11 and 12
were taken by Elisabeth Stanbrook.

Front Cover: Inscribed stone at Sticklepath

Contents

Illustrations

Front Cover: Bennet's Cross

Preface

In the series of articles on *The Stones of Dartmoor and Their Story* only those monuments belonging to the pre-historic period were dealt with. But there are other antiquities on the Moor of equal interest with the dwellings and sepulchres of early man, though of a later time, and a few examples of these we now propose briefly to notice. They may be classed as early historic and medieval, and embrace a variety of objects, among others hill-forts and bridges, ancient crosses, the roofless blowing-houses of the tinners, shepherds' huts, and manorial boundstones. The first named, the hill camp, sometimes belongs to the pre-historic period, but as those surrounding Dartmoor do not appear to be of such early date, it was thought well not to include them in the account of the ruder remains, and they therefore find a place here.

WILLIAM CROSSING

Introduction

The name William Crossing will be familiar with all those who have an interest in Dartmoor. Born in Plymouth in 1847, he had an early introduction to the Moor when his family holidays took him to Roborough. Crossing's love of Dartmoor developed and remained with him for the rest of his life. Many of those years were spent recording both the information that he obtained from the moormen and his own observations, so that when he died in 1928, he left behind a wealth of literature for future generations to digest.

Crossing's *Dartmoor's Early Historic and Medieval Remains* is but one small part of his literary output. Under the title *Early Historic and Medieval Remains on Dartmoor*, it first appeared as a series of articles that were syndicated in a number of West Country newspapers, including the *Western Morning News* in 1905. Printed here for the first time in book form, it is a sequel to the recently published book, *Stones of Dartmoor and Their Story*, which also appeared as a series of articles in the same newspapers, in 1904.

Dartmoor's Early Historic and Medieval Remains provides a fascinating account of the Moor's granite, employed by man for his wide range of uses. Boundary stones, crosses, bridges, tumble-down dwellings and the remains of the once flourishing tin-mining industry are all to be found on Dartmoor, as symbols of a bygone age. As Crossing so aptly says, "The rambler over the waste will not fail to come across many more, and if he loves that which is old, the discovery will lend an additional interest to his wanderings."

1

Strongholds of Forgotten Heroes

Fingle Gorge

Along a narrow path on the northern side of the deep Gorge of Fingle, three men, clad in the skins of beasts, are rapidly making their way. It is early morn, and the sun is not yet high enough to penetrate into the depths of the vale, where the Teign, hidden beneath a canopy of green, is heard forcing a passage between the rocks which he, in times of flood, has himself brought down from the solitudes of Dartmoor. Drops of dew hang from the coarse grass and heather that partly cover the hillside, and a thin, fleecy cloud steals slowly from below to kiss the glistening pearls. Then it rolls upwards, but finds no hiding-place, for the young day has filled the hollows with his light, and it is driven still further up, but only to lose itself upon the scented air. In certain spots no grass and heather are seen, but only scrubby oaks thrusting themselves from stony ground, as though struggling to rise to greet the morning sun, lest he should be forgetful, and neglect to gild them with his beams. By-and-bye thick undergrowth covers the scarp, and here one of the men leaves his fellows and passes down towards the river. The other two force their way through the wood, and presently find themselves on the steep side of a heather-covered hill, that descends sheer into the Teign. On its summit is a camp of great size, approached from the spot at which the men have arrived by a narrow, winding path. By means of this they speedily reach the ramparts, and enter unchallenged, for they are known. As yet only a few of those within the fort have risen; the rest are wrapped in slumber. But on the tidings brought by the early visitors becoming known, sleepers are awakened, men run hither and thither, and sentinels are posted at various points. It has been discovered by the scouts that a large force of invaders are advancing towards the Fingle Gorge, and the men who are to hold the pass are preparing to receive them. The name of the fortified hill is Prestonbury, and those who will defend it are Britons.

High above the river, on the further side of the valley, and looking down even on the lofty Prestonbury, is another fort, today called Cranbrook Castle. And here, some time before the messenger sent to warn them is able to reach it, the men are also astir, for the watchers have seen their brothers gathering as though for battle and have spread the alarm. Further down the valley is a third fort, now known as Wooston Castle; those who hold it have already learnt of the advancing foe from the man who left his comrades when they had plunged into the undergrowth. If, as is supposed, the enemy's intention is to penetrate into the hill country, where the Dart takes his rise, he will attempt to pass through the gorge, and must be looked for at its lower end which opens towards the rising sun. Upon the men behind the entrenchments of Wooston, and Cranbrook, and Prestonbury devolves the task of repelling him; it is theirs to see that the Roman eagle shall not float over Western Damnonia.

The hours pass by, but nothing is seen of the foe. The day is fair, the sun shines in an unclouded sky, and Nature speaks only of tranquility. The birds sing their joyous songs, the whispering breeze is answered by the dreamy humming of insects, the coney sits by her burrow, fearless of danger; everything tells of peace and happiness. It is only in the hearts of man that there is strife.

Scouts come into the camps, but they bring no tidings of the expected foe; he is nowhere to be seen. The drowsy afternoon glides slowly away, and at length the sun is seen dropping towards the higher end of the defile, beyond which old Cosdon lifts up his Titanic bulk. Lower and lower the red sun sinks; shadows appear between the folding hills; they deepen, and the gorge is wrapped in gloom. The bright robe that the long valley put on with the dawn is exchanged for a black mantle. The only sound that breaks the stillness is the voice of the Teign that comes up from its depths into which the stars look, where an opening in the foliage that enshrouds the river leaves its bosom bare.

Suddenly a jarring note is struck; man, too often ready to destroy the harmony of Nature, breaks in upon the stillness of the night. Loud shouts are heard down the valley, and the men of Prestonbury and Cranbrook know that their brothers of Wooston have encountered the foe. From their massive ramparts of stone and turf they move quickly downward, the light of the newly-risen moon enabling them to follow the secret paths through the oak woods that descend to the stream. When they reach the foot of Wooston their brothers are already engaged with the foe. They throw themselves into the fray, and soon it becomes evident that victory will not lie with the trained soldiers. The hardy son of Damnonia is animated with that which finds no place in the heart of the Roman. He fights for his home, his country; the Roman has nothing but the lust of conquest as an incentive. And so it comes about that the rude men who threw up the high banks, and dug the deep entrenchments on the steeps above the Gorge of Fingle become the victors in the fight with those who would take from them their land. At first the foe gives way but slowly, but the Damnonii press onward so fiercely that at length he is constrained to gather his forces and retire.

When the sun again looks upon the gorge it sees it still in the hands of its old possessors. If the Roman would yet seek to penetrate into the highlands of the Dart, let him find another way that shall bring him there. But whichever path he chooses the Damnonian will dispute it.

Prestonbury is the largest of the camps in the Dartmoor borderland, and covers, it is said, no less than twenty-five acres. It occupies the summit of a great hill that rises precipitously from the northern bank of the Teign, immediately below Fingle Bridge. Being almost inaccessible on this side, it was unnecessary to fortify it strongly here, and consequently we find that the vallum was not thrown up to a great height. But on the northern side of the hill it was different; here the vallum is very high, and combined with the other defences must have rendered the fort impregnable. There was one entrance on this side; another on the east; and a third on the west. Eastward of the main portion of the camp are two strong outworks, each consisting of a rampart and a ditch, and still further east traces of other fortifications also occur. Although overlooked by Cranbrook the distance was too great to allow of its defenders being harmed by arrows or sling-stones discharged from there, supposing that fort to be captured by an enemy. With both in the hands of the Briton it is difficult to see how the pass could be forced. If Wooston failed to prevent the foe pressing up the gorge, Cranbrook and Prestonbury would still confront him, and in an attempt to penetrate further he would find himself between two fires.

Great as man's work has been at Prestonbury, Nature's has been greater. She was the engineer that threw up the huge scarp, defying by its height and steepness the assaults of the foe, were he ever so strong; she placed the huge hill where its crest should command the valley, and the approach of an invader be seen, came he from the east or from the west. To man belongs only the credit of adding to Nature's work, so that he might be able to hold the hill against an enemy, and in the formation of his ditches and mounds he has given much evidence of his skill. But his labours at Prestonbury ceased ages ago; the work of Nature still continues. Every year she covers the hill with a glory far greater than that with which it was crowned even in the hour of its holders' proudest victory. One was the glory of war; her's the glory of peace. For the crimson

11

flood that once stained its slopes she substitutes a purple mantle; and for the groans of wounded men the carols of birds rejoicing in the golden light of the summer day, or the mellowed sweetness of autumn.

From the well-known Fingle Bridge at the foot of Prestonbury, a zigzag road ascends through the woods that here clothe the side of the hill, to Uppacott Down, above the south bank of the Teign, and it is on this common that Cranbrook Castle is placed. The site of this entrenched circumvallation was most happily chosen, both for purposes of observation and defence. Rising some seven hundred feet above the river, it stands on ground higher than that occupied by any other camp in this locality, and consequently must have been a point of considerable importance. But the wonderful view on every hand is what will chiefly strike the beholder who climbs its ruined vallum today. From Cosdon, which here shows itself to wonderful advantage, the frontier hills of Eastern Dartmoor are seen extending towards the south, and the picture gives the visitor some idea of the vastness of that region. In other directions the cultivated country rolls away as far as the eye can reach.

Cranbrook Castle was carefully examined early in the last century by Mr. W. T. P. Shortt, who has left a most interesting record of his investigations. It was also visited by Lysons when the Devonshire volume of the "Magna Britannia" was being prepared, and according to his measurements the camp covers a space of about six or seven acres. It is of irregular circular form, and consists of a rampart of earth and stones, which, on the south side, is of considerable height. Here also there is a double ditch, and on the west side a single one. Such a defence was not necessary on the north side, the hill being then very steep. Fragments of pottery and also sling-stones have been discovered here during recent years. Unfortunately Cranbrook has suffered at the hands of the spoliator. The rampart has served as a quarry for the road mender, and much of it had even been removed in Mr. Shortt's time. Since then the work of destruction has been occasionally resumed; nevertheless, Cranbrook is still a good example of ancient castrametation, and being placed on a commanding hill, and in close proximity to the romantic Fingle Gorge, offers attractions both to the antiquary and to the seeker after the beautiful in Nature.

About a mile and a half from Cranbrook is Wooston Castle, the remains of which present features of even greater interest than those exhibited by the former, or by its neighbour Prestonbury. But unlike them, it is not placed on the summit of a hill, and, consequently, does not at first impress the beholder in the same way as they do. The camp is, however, situated at a considerable height above the Teign, and above a tree-hidden cliff, and if not impregnable from the downs behind it, was certainly so on the side of the pass, and that the primary object of its erection was to command this, there can be little doubt. Like Prestonbury and Cranbrook, the works are slight on those sides where Nature has already provided a defence. On the south, where it would be most open to attack, the rampart is very high, and the ditch in front of it of great depth. In form it is an irregular oval, and the vallum is composed of earth. Some outer works form an additional defence, and a ditch running down the hill has been thought to be a way by which the river could be reached unobserved. Of these three forts commanding the Gorge of the Teign, Cranbrook may be regarded as being the oldest.

Another interesting border camp is Hembury Castle, near Buckfast, not entirely on account of its state, but also for the beauty of its situation. According to a tradition attaching to it. Hembury was once held by a tribe of men who were said to have come from the North. This, however, must not be taken as pointing to a Scandinavian occupation of the hill. In the story the holders of the fort are characterised as oppressors, and were feared and hated by the peasantry. That they should be described as coming from the North, a quarter that has always borne an evil reputation as the abode of malicious spirits, is, therefore, not a matter of surprise. The men of the Dart Valley suffered much from the marauding bands that came down from Hembury; they found themselves unable to prevent the raids that were made upon them, so numerous were the strangers. For long this continued, and none could devise means of relief. But what man could not do woman, says the legend, was able to accomplish. The wives and daughters of the peasantry suffered themselves to be captured, and taken to the camp on the hill. In honour of what they deemed their victory, a feast was proclaimed by the men of Hembury. Strong drink was freely indulged in, and after the banquet the merrymakers lay about in a state of helpless intoxication. Then the women stealthily possessed themselves of the daggers of their captors, and buried them in the throats of their owners. Thus was the Dart valley freed from the presence of those who had so long oppressed it.

Hembury Castle is placed on a tree-clad hill above the Dart, between Holne Bridge and Buckfast. It is said to cover an area of about seven acres, and in shape is an irregular oblong. There is a deep ditch and a high vallum, but is it difficult to make a thorough examination of this ancient fort, as the trees have encroached upon its ramparts, and hide much of it from view.

The conspicuous eminence of Brent Hill has also been fortified. The remains of an earthern vallum and a ditch may be seen on its southern slope, at no great distance below the summit. Its northern side is precipitous and craggy, and here no artificial defences were needed.

Near the road leading from Plympton to Shaugh Common are the remains of a fort known as Boringdon Camp. The rampart encloses a space of about four acres, and seems to have been formerly surrounded by a ditch, though the vestiges of it are very slight. It commands the estuary of the Plym, and was probably an encampment of some importance.

Few hills are better known than the church-crowned Brent Tor. The little sanctuary that renders it so conspicuous has been standing between six and seven hundred years, but centuries before its foundations were laid man had thrown up his defensive works there. The ditches are still in existence, and, like those in similar situations, are placed so as to guard that part of the hill from which the summit might most readily have been reached. On the other side of it there is a precipice, and the primitive engineers were here saved the trouble of fortifying it.

Of an earlier date than either of the border camps noticed, unless, perhaps it be Cranbrook, is the circumvallation on White Tor, or Whittor, as it is called, above Cudlipp Town Down, in the parish of Petertavy. While the others probably belong to the early centuries of the Christian era, this enclosure, there can hardly be a doubt, dates from pre-historic times. It is the only thing of its kind on the Moor, for not one of the other pounds there occupies a situation suitable for a fort. This enclosure crowns a prominent hill, and whether we are to regard it as a camp, or whether it is merely an ordinary pound occupying an unusual site, it is certain that for the purposes of defence the latter is an admirable one. The vallum is in part formed by the rocks of the Tor, and when in its complete state must have been of considerable strength. Within it are some decayed hut circles, and numerous flints have been found in and around them.

At the eastern end of that part of the Moor included within the bounds of Okehampton Park is East Hill, and here, near the beautiful Ashbury Tor, are the remains of some entrenchments and high banks, which are known in the neighbourhood as The Camp, but which at one time bore the name of The Danes' Battery. A plan of them was made in 1840 by the Rev. H. G. Fothergill, rector of Belstone, who considered that he saw in the remains British, Roman and Danish work. That the Danes built any part of the camp is more than doubtful, but that the Roman after having wrested it from the Briton, occupied it, and added to it, is not improbable. The fort overlooks the valley of the East Ockment, and, as in the other examples we have noticed, is comparatively undefended on the side where the nature of the ground would prevent the approach of an enemy.

But the visitor to this hill will find something more to attract him than speculations concerning this ancient fort and its builders, unless his antiquarian tastes crowd out all else. But this is hardly likely to be so, and therefore we will take it for granted that the beauties of Halstock Cleave, and of the Tor that looks down upon them, do not escape him. If he does not find sufficient in the camp to hold him interested, he will certainly discover this in its surroundings.

With the exception of the remains at White Tor and at East Hill, no hill fort exists on Dartmoor. Those we have here briefly noticed are found at a short distance from it, but within the borderland, and having regard to their probable purpose, that of the defence of the highlands, belong more to the land of stream and tor than to the country of living green that surrounds it.

2

Graven on Granite

Yard's Gate or Seven Star's Gate

The long upright stone reared by man in his ruder state discloses only a small part of its secret. When, as is often the case, it is found in connection with interments, there is sufficient reason for believing it to be a memorial of the dead; when such objects are absent we may perhaps not be wrong in regarding it as having been set up in commemoration of some victory. But more than this we cannot know. The tall shaft does not tell us what the deed was that it was

15

intended to bring to men's minds, nor, if it marks a burial place, who it is that lies beneath the turf. But when man became more civilised he was not content that the only witness of the event, or of the person whose memory he wished to perpetuate, should be an unhewn stone. He covered his monument with carvings, which though often conveying no meaning to us, were once readily recognised, and represented, it may be, the battles of some great conqueror. Or he placed the name of his departed hero upon the stone, that he should not be forgotten; that he being dead might yet speak. The unwrought menhir became the inscribed pillar, and its message has been handed down through the ages.

On Dartmoor we do not find any inscribed stones. A few exist on its borders, and may consequently be regarded as belonging to that region, but on the Moor itself the monuments are all of a primitive type. When Roman civilisation advanced westward it did not penetrate into the hill country, and it is highly probable, nay, almost certain, that the stone man continued to inhabit it long after he had disappeared from the lowlands, and that he there observed customs that had elsewhere become things of the past.

One of the proclivities of civilised man of the genus idler is that of carving his name or initials in public places, as on trees by the wayside, or in parks, on the backs of seats, or other objects that can be cut into without much effort. This proclivity he inherits; it is one that has been indulged in from the earliest times. When Bill Stumps engraved his name, doubtless with much labour, upon the stone discovered by Mr. Pickwick, he was only doing what the men of the Prætorian cohort had done in the guardroom on the Palatine Hill; what was done at Pompeii, and what has been done by the Arab, the Indian, the African, the native of Peru, and by rude tribes in many parts of the world, as ancient inscriptions and rock carvings abundantly testify. But every man on Dartmoor does not appear even to have engaged in this almost universal practice; he has left nothing graven on the granite of its thousand hills; nothing cut on its rocks that shall afford a clue to what he was, or speak to us of the mighty deeds he accomplished. Some writing on the stone, indeed, there is. But it is modern, and possesses no interest for us. It is the work of an antiquary who some century since formed the idea of covering the rocks in the Cowsic, under Bear Down, with inscriptions in the form of couplets, addressed to various poets and mythical personages, some of them to be written in the bardic characters as given in Davies' "Celtic Researches." This design, likely to lead to more confusion than the work that engaged the attention of the Pickwick Club, was, however, carried out only in part. The achievement was recorded; a circumstance which has perhaps been the means of saving many the trouble of endeavouring to show that the letters were cut at some very remote period, and at the same time has spared us many a laboured disquisition.

The inscribed stones in the Dartmoor borderland appear to date from early Christian times, though there are one or two that may possibly be older. Those existing on the northern verge of the Moor, chiefly at Tavistock and near Sticklepath, are supposed to be indicative of a religious awakening following upon the arrival in the western peninsula of missionaries from the South of Ireland, and to belong to the 6th or 7th century. The three fine examples

16

preserved in the vicarage garden at Tavistock have been frequently described. One of them, which was removed from West-street about the year 1784, where it had served as a paving-stone, bears an inscription in Latin showing it to have been erected to Nepranus, son of Condevus. Another, brought in 1831 from the village of Buckland Monachorum, is to the memory of Sabinus, son of Maceodechetus. The third was discovered in the lane leading from the village named to Roborough Down, and was brought to Tavistock in 1868; it is commemorative of Dobunnius Faber, son of Enabarrus. The latter is a particularly interesting stone, as the inscription appears not only in Latin, but also in the primitive characters known as Oghams, found on ancient monuments in Ireland. This, together with the names, which have been considered to be Irish, points to the presence here of people of that country. The name on the Buckland stone has also an Irish sound, the prefixes "mac" and "o" both appearing in it. But with regard to the stone found at Tavistock there is little beyond probability to enable us to connect it with those who first Christianised this part of our island. This, however, we think is sufficiently strong to justify us in doing so.

There is a small stone now acting as a gatepost at the head of the lane leading to Yards Down, near Will Farm, in the parish of Peter Tavy, on which are some curious markings that resemble letters. As far as can be made out there appears to be the letter T in one line, and in another S C, and lower down the shaft a second C. The stone is evidently ancient, and does not seem to have been a bond mark, as the letters have not only no meaning in such a connection, but are not disposed in such a manner as we should expect to find on an object of that kind. The gate is known as Yards Gate, or Yards Down Gate, but is sometimes called, in allusion to the markings on the stone, Seven Stars Gate.

By the side of the Okehampton road, northward of Prewley Moor, is a fine stone cross rather over eight feet in height. That it was formed out of an ancient menhir we shall hardly doubt when we find that its arms are so short that they project no more than about two and a half inches. On the shaft is an inscription, in three lines, which is not easy to decipher. This, however, has been done by the Rev. S. Baring-Gould, whose rendering shows it to be similar in character to the inscriptions on the stones at Tavistock.

Built into the wall by the side of the drive leading to the old Belstone rectory, is a stone about four feet in height bearing some curious incised markings. A line runs part way up its centre, crossed by another near the top, the latter forming the segment of a circle. Above this is a complete circle, about fifteen inches in diameter, having the figure of a cross within it. The edges of the stone appear to have been broken, and a part of it near the base on one side is missing. Many years ago I learnt that this stone had been removed from Belstone Church, in 1861, during a time when some alterations were in progress there, but I could never gain a clear account of this.

A short distance westward of Sticklepath, a lane, which leads to Bude Farm, diverges from the Okehampton highway, and here, too, is a stone having some curious markings. On its northern face, among other imperfect figures, a St. Andrew's cross, with a circle above it, can be distinguished. On the eastern and southern faces are also lines and semi-circles, but on its western face nothing is to be seen. The stone is rather more than four and a half feet in height.

But the finest example of an inscribed stone in that immediate neighbourhood is to be seen on the verge of the common at the entrance to the village of Sticklepath. It is a foot higher than the one just noticed, and also much larger, while the figures upon it are more boldly cut. What these represent cannot be determined, but two St. Andrew's crosses can be plainly seen, and there is also a Latin cross in relief. When the road near it was being made, many years since, this stone was unfortunately undermined and fell down, but was soon replaced.

At Lustleigh is a stone bearing an inscription which has been read as "Catvidoc Conrino." It is rather unfortunate that this old memorial of a far-off day should have been suffered to lie for years in the south porch of the church, where passing feet would do more in a decade towards obliterating the letters than time would be likely to accomplish in a century. If, as is likely, this stone dates from a period before the introduction of Christianity, it may perhaps be claimed that such a situation was not altogether an inappropriate one. It would be emblematical of bringing the heathen within the fold, and at the same time would tend to wipe him out altogether.

According to the notes to Carrington's "Dartmoor" there formerly existed an inscribed stone at Stowford, near Ivybridge. About the year 1824 it was removed, and after being suitably cut, was used as a step at the chapel in that village. The writer of the notes also says that another stone, covered with carved work, was about that time to be seen in the bed of the Erme. No description of these stones is given, but the connection in which they are mentioned leads to the supposition that they were of that character.

Another stone, and perhaps the most interesting of all that have been found on the borders of the Moor, is that sometimes referred to as the Fardle Stone. Unfortunately this is no longer to be seen on, or near, the spot where it formerly stood; to examine this stone it will be necessary to make a long journey. It was discovered many years ago near Fardle, on the road between Ivybridge and Cornwood, and having been brought to the notice of Sir Edward Smirke was, through his instrumentality, removed to the British Museum. While Devonshiremen will be gratified that their county should be represented in the national treasure-house, they will probably feel that they are paying rather a high price for the privilege when this entails the removal of their stone monuments, and will be inclined to think that those who wish to examine them should come where they are. Like the stone found near Roborough Down, and now at Tavistock, the Fardle Stone bears an inscription in the Ogham character. There are two inscriptions in Roman letters, one on each side of the shaft, and, as in the case of the Buckland stone, we also have here the prefix "mac," or rather "maq." Thus we know to what race the man, or men, belonged, who are commemorated by this lettered pillar, and the period when he, or they, lived and worked here. We are pointed to a Gaelic tribe, and to the early days of Christianising effort.

18

3

The Symbol of the Christian Faith

Huntingdon Cross

From the rude menhir to the inscribed pillar was a natural transition, and, having regard to the course of events, from the inscribed pillar to the cross one not less natural. Their purposes were much the same; both the unhewn and the graven monoliths were memorial stones, and that the cross was often so there can be no doubt. And they each had a message for man; that proclaimed by the tall upright stone, rough from its native bed, it may well be, not only told of one departed, but also pointed to the spirit land; the graven pillar was more articulate; the cross, though bearing no inscription, spoke with a yet louder voice, was even eloquent, and delivered a message clear as the sun at noon. Among the various monuments on Dartmoor perhaps none possesses a greater interest than this.

Though the veil that hangs between us and the far-away time when the stone man dwelt upon the Moor does not altogether hide his doings from us; though the meaning of his granite rows and circles is sufficiently evident, save when obscured by extravagant theories concerning them; there is yet much that the past does not disclose. But a light shines upon the cross. We are in no doubt concerning the manner of men who reared it, and we know what prompted them to do so. These emblems of an object once linked with shame, but now glorious, are as an open book, and if we cannot read their individual histories, we can, looking upon them, read that of an event the results of which will not end with Time.

The crosses of Dartmoor particularly appeal to us. They are found in wild and solitary places, and tell us how those who set them up were mindful of the wayfarer, and desired not only that he should be guided across the wide heath, but also that he should be directed to a better country, perhaps far-off, or it might be that he stood upon its confines. In the sheltered valley they are seen, where summer winds whisper, or faintly sigh at night-fall; by the stream that softly murmurs under a sunny sky, or rushes impetuously onward swollen by the brooks that pour from rain-soaked hills; near the rugged tor, gilded by the rising sun, or looming darkly through the mist; on the lofty hill, standing boldly up with outstretched arms, a sign to all. Most of the Dartmoor crosses were erected as guides to the green paths that led over the waste, while others were bond-marks, and in some instances we find them serving both these purposes. They are plain Latin crosses, some being very rudely fashioned, and even those seen in the border villages, though of a different character, do not exhibit any elaborate workmanship.

It is noticeable that in the northern district of Dartmoor none of those objects are to be found, with the exception of one at Fitz's Well, in Okehampton Park, although several important paths exist there; while in other parts of the Moor many examples are to be seen. But this is easily accounted for. On the borders of southern Dartmoor were four important religious houses —Buckfast, Plympton, Buckland, and Tavistock — and it may be seen that the chief tracks in the south quarter of the Moor lead from one to the other of these. That they were used by the monks is therefore certain; in fact, the most important of them still bears the name of the Abbots' Way, and we can consequently well understand why the stones set up to mark the direction of these, in places, ill-defined roads, should have been given the form of the cross. Around the northern part of Dartmoor no abbeys existed, and thus there were were no monks's paths. The tracks found there were those chiefly used by the farm settlers in the valleys of the Dart and Wallabrook as a means of communication with Lydford and Okehampton. A few stones they set up where they deemed them necessary, but they were not concerned in fashioning them into crosses.

20

The Abbots' Way led from Buckfast Abbey, on the eastern side of the Moor, to Tavistock Abbey, founded in 981, and Buckland Abbey, founded three hundred years later, on the western side of it. The abbey at Buckfast is sometimes spoken of as having been founded in 1137, but this was really the date of its enlargement; there is mention of a religious house there in the Domesday Survey, and as it even then had large possessions it is probable that its foundation was much earlier. But, however this may be, we can hardly doubt that the path on the Moor dates at least from the latter part of the 11th century, since a direct means of communication would certainly be formed between Buckfast and Tavistock. Two of the crosses on the line of this ancient way are named in 1557 as boundary stones, but it is highly probable that they were merely adapted to this purpose, and that their original intention was to mark the path. These were Huntingdon Cross and a cross at Buckland Ford, of which only the former now exists. This stands just within the Forest boundary, at the point where the Avon receives the Wellabrook; the latter, according to the record in which it is named, stood near a shallow crossing-place on a little tributary of the Avon, and pointed the way by which the path ascended the hill rising between that river and the springs of Red Lake. These crosses are referred to in an account of an Inquisition regarding the bounds of Brent Moor, and two others are there also spoken of, one erected on a cairn at Three Barrows, and another on Western Whitaburrow, of each of which portions only now remain. These four crosses are certified by the commissioners to have been set up by them, but it does not, of course, necessarily follow that they were then erected for the first time; indeed, there is evidence, apart from the probability of Huntingdon Cross and the cross at Buckland Ford having originally been set up by the monks, that this was not the case. The cross on Three Barrows, for instance, is shown on the old map of Dartmoor now in the Albert Memorial Museum at Exeter, as Hobajon's Cross, the name by which it is still known, or, rather, according to the moorman's pronunciation, Hoppyjone's. Even if the map be of no earlier date than the Inquisition in question, the fact of the cross having a name affixed to it would certainly show that it was an object that would be recognised by such. The commissioners also certified that the crosses bore the words, "Bunda de Brentmoor," but if so these could not have been cut upon the stone, for no trace of an inscription is to be found on either of them now.

Siward's Cross, or, as it is more often called, Nun's Cross, the fine example a short distance southward of Princetown, stands on the Tavistock branch of the Abbots' Way, which diverges from the Buckland path at Broad Rock, near the head of the Erme. On this part of the old path there could never have been much traffic, as a more direct way from the spot where the paths diverged to the abbey on the Tavy was to be found. The path itself shows this. From Broad Rock the way is well worn down the hill to Plym Steps, and on towards Sheepston; but from that point to Siward's Cross there are only faint traces of it, and in places it is lost entirely. The path shown on the Ordnance map as the Abbots' Way is not the old monks' path, but a mine and peat road of comparatively recent date. While Siward's Cross served as a guide to this old way, it may have been that its original purpose was that of a bond-mark. It stands on the Forest boundary line, and its name is said to be derived from Siward, Earl of Northumberland, who held land here, perhaps a grant of this part of the Forest, in the Confessor's time. But about this we cannot be certain, for the Abbey of Tavistock having been founded prior to the close of the 10th century, the monks may have erected it as a guide, and it may have been merely adapted as a bond-mark by Siward. The monks of Buckland certainly only adapted it when they engraved the name of their abbey upon it, for it is mentioned forty years before that house was founded.

Siward's Cross also stands on the line of a track which I have traced across the Forest by means of the objects we are now noticing. This path ran from Buckland to the eastern side of the Moor, with a branch from it, forming an alternative route to Buckfast. It entered the Moor near Dousland, where stood Yanedone Cross, what was probably the base of it being now to be seen in a gateway not far from the Manor Hotel. The track then went on by Lowery to the Mew, which is crossed, and passed up the side of the valley of the Newleycombe Lake, at the head of which Siward's Cross was reached. It then ran down the higher part of the Swincombe Valley under Fox Tor, and so on over Ter Hill to Horse Ford, when the Buckfast branch diverged. The easterly path then ran down the Wobrook, and through Huccaby to Dartmeet. In my book, "The Ancient Stone Crosses of Dartmoor and Its Borderland," I have described the crosses that marked this track, but I am now able to add two that have come to light since the last edition of the book appeared. One of these probably stood between Lowery and Lether Tor Bridge, near a gate still known as Cross Gate. The cross itself is to be seen in the wall belonging to the farm below it. The other, which consists of the head only, was discovered a few years ago by Lieut. Lennon-Goldsmith, who, in his letter to me respecting it, points out that it is directly in a line between Siward's Cross and Childe's Tomb, and that its existence is confirmatory of my opinion that the crosses in this part of the Forest were set up in order to mark a pathway. The cross was found on the ground, and in a rock near it was the socket in which it had formerly been fixed. It was replaced by Lieut. Lennon-Goldsmith, and properly secured with cement.

The cross at Childe's Tomb, below Fox Tor, disappeared many years ago. In 1826 it lay on the ground, broken, by the side of the ruined monument celebrated in Dartmoor tradition that vandalistic hands had destroyed. What afterwards became of it is not known, but I think it probable that the head of a cross which was found in 1881 is a portion of it. This I observed in that year in a corner of Fox Tor Newtake, a spot to which a name has since been given by a Scotch shepherd, and which perhaps reflects some of his experiences there when sheep gathering during inclement weather. He called it Mount Misery. When I saw the head of the cross it had just been unearthed by some workmen, who had walled up a gateway there. I endeavoured to get it fixed on the tomb under Fox Tor when the restoration (?) of that monument was effected, but I was not successful. A new cross was deemed more fitting. A good example of these granite memorials of a past day stands in this newtake corner, and others are to be found on Ter Hill near by.

As a boundary cross the rude stone on the lofty Hameldon is not wanting in interest. It is formed out of a slab rather over four feet in height. It bears a modern date, which was cut when some bond-marks were renewed about half a century ago.

On Whitchurch Down is probably one of the oldest of the crosses of the Moor. Though it stands on the Abbots' Way, there is reason to believe that it is of much earlier date than that path. The most important among the Dartmoor examples is the cross referred to more than six hundred years ago as Smalacumbacrosse, and which in all probability is identical with Marchants Cross, near Meavy. This not only marked the Abbots' Way, but also a track running from Plympton Priory to Sampford Spiney, a possession of that house, as well as forming a bond-mark of the lands granted by the Countess of Devon to Buckland Abbey.

When my account of the crosses of Dartmoor first appeared, now more than twenty years ago, a number of them were lying broken and neglected. It is pleasing to know that attention having been directed to these, many have since been cared for, and, both on the lonely heath and in the border village, are now to be seen erect.

4

Bond-marks

Gray Weather Boundary Stone

In a district like that to which the name of Dartmoor now attaches, where an ancient Forest is entirely surrounded by extensive commons belonging to different parishes, the whole of them being unenclosed, we naturally find a large number of objects marking their bounds. The following remarks are confined chiefly to the objects themselves rather than to the boundaries which they define, many of the latter having already been noticed in previous articles.

The earliest recorded boundaries in connection with the Moor are those erroneously stated by Risdon and others to form the limits of the Venville men's tenures, but which are really those of some lands extending from Ashburton to Lustleigh, and apparently to North Bovey, which were supposed by the late Mr. J. B. Davidson to have been connected with the See of Exeter. Many of the names enumerated it would now be impossible to identify, but the objects marking the bounds included stones, streams, a well, and a ditch. The record of Dartmoor boundaries that comes next in point of time is the return to the Perambulation of the Forest made in 1240, of which several copies exist. These metes and bounds are, of course, of greater importance than any in the moorland district, and though we do not know when they were first fixed, were certainly recognised a century earlier than the date named, and the probability is that they were determined long prior to that time. The objects by which this boundary was marked were partly natural and partly artificial. Among the former we have hills, tors, streams, with their sources and confluences; and a ford, besides which mention is also made of a turbary through which the line is drawn. The artificial bond-marks comprise a building, a path, two stream-works, two stones (one a menhir, and the other probably of the same character), and a cross, this latter being Siward's Cross, to which reference has already been made (Chapter 3). These belonged to the Forest, for, according to Forest law the objects marking the boundary were regarded as being within it. At the same time it is evident that only part of an object was sometimes inside the Forest, if it was so specified. We see this in the case of Mis Tor, where the line is drawn through the group of rocks, one part of the tor thus being outside the Forest, and this is set forth by the perambulators of 1240, who carry the boundary "per mediam Mystor," as well as in the charter of the Countess of Devon, of 1291, where the line is drawn from "Mistorpanna," evidently the rock in which is the remarkable basin. The jury who surveyed the Forest bounds in 1609 recognised for this, for in their return at the court held at Okehampton, they give the boundary line as running "through the midst of Mistorr Moore to a rocke called Mistorrpan." But the land referred to does not seem to have been always recognised by those whose lands abutted on the Forest, for in more than one instance the bond-stones of the latter are placed in the centre of the object marking the Forest boundary. Thus on Ryder's Hill, there are two stones in the middle of the dilapidated cairn, one of them marking the limits of the parish of Holne, and the other those of Buckfastleigh; and the cross set up on Western Whitaburrow, as named in the article on those objects, is another instance, while others might be given.

The four quarters into which the forest is divided were also defined in places by bond marks, consisting of upright stones. It does not appear there were ever many of these, but a copy of an old map in my possession shows that more formerly existed than are now to be seen.

Next in importance to the boundary of the Forest are the bounds of its purlieus, or commons that encircle it . These are also parish bounds, and are usually viewed periodically. The bond-marks, chiefly consisting of granite posts, are carried from the verge of the common out to the Forest, a distance in some cases of several miles. Thus a number of bond-stones stand on the Forest line (or are supposed to) that have nothing to do with marking it, and have never been named as bounds in any of the surveys of the latter. In those instances where these stones do not stand on the true boundary line of the Forest, it will invariably be found that the common bounds have been thrust out, and that an encroachment on the Forest has taken place. Near Western

Whitaburrow, the cairn on which Petre's Cross formerly stood, is a stone, called Little Petre. It marks what is now claimed as the boundary of Brent Moor, although the Perambulation and Surveys all show that the part of the hill on the brow of which it stands belongs to the Forest. Similar instances occur on Danger Plain, in the northern part of the moor, at Taw Plain, on Metherell Hill, and in other places.

Sometimes it is found that the commons, in addition to being marked off from each other by bondstones, are also themselves divided in a similar way. These stones usually define the bounds of manors. Other stones again mark the bounds of mineral rights. There is one of this kind on the eastern side of Cosdon, near a small clatter known as the Rabbits' Holt. Miners' bounds are sometimes marked by a few small stones, set up in a peculiar manner, or by little heaps of soil, known as stannaburrows, while workings of an earlier date are found marked off by low reaves. There are also some boundary-stones defining the ground over which the right to cut peat has been granted by the Duchy to various companies, and many others that mark the bounds of warrens.

One of the objects alluded to as standing on the Forest line, but having been set up really to mark the bounds of a common, is the Wellabrook Stone, which stands at the head of the Western Wellabrook, a tributary of the Avon. It is rather higher than the stones usually erected for the purpose, and has the letter B cut upon it, as being a bondmark of Buckfastleigh Moor. Another is the Outer U Stone, on the left bank of Red Lake, which is supposed to mark the limits of Ugborough Moor, but which is really situated some distance within the Forest line. It is the last stone of a long row extending from near Three Barrows to the Forest, and is so called in consequence of bearing the initial letter of the name of the Moor the bounds of which it marks. Others in the row are similarly inscribed, and one of these, situated between Three Barrows and Stony Bottom, is always known as the U Stone by the moormen. From below Three Barrows, in the other direction, to the summit of Wetherdon Hill, this boundary, which separates Ugborough Moor from Harford Moor, is formed by a stone row, the ancient monument having thus been adapted to a purpose, in all probability, very different from its original one.

Another mark on the Forest line, as at present recognised, is Broad Rock, a boundary of Blachford Manor, on which, besides the name of the stone, the letters B B are inscribed. Near it is another bond-mark, of the same manor, and having A Head cut upon it. A stands for Arme, the old form of Erme, and the one always used by the moormen when speaking of that river. In two instances rock-streams, known generally as clatters, or clitters, form bond-marks of commons on the Forest line. Thus, on the east side we have Hewthorn Clitter, on the bounds of Gidleigh Commmon; and in the north, Curtory Clitters, on Okehampton Common, or rather on a part of the Moor now included in that common, but which there can be no doubt was once within the Forest. A reave marks the Forest bounds north and south of Siward's Cross, and on Shovel Down, in the neighbourhood of Chagford, it is defined in several places by means of rude stone remains. About three miles to the north of this down is

Whitemoor Stone, which, although not mentioned in any Perambulation, is evidently of some antiquity, and stands on the line of the Forest, although this is not now drawn from it towards the north in the direction it formerly ran. An important bond-mark that does not receive mention in the Surveys has been removed within comparatively recent years. This was the Rundle Stone, between North Hisworthy Tor and Mis Tor, of which mention is first made in 1702.

As in the case of Broad Rock, flat rocks, or stones, sometimes form bond-marks, but the majority of these consist of small granite pillars. To many of these names attach, and some of them are rather curious. On the down, near the green path leading from the head of Church-lane, above the village of Widecombe, to Gore Hill, is a manor boundary stone known as Aaron's Knock. Whether the name is a fanciful one, or whether it is a corruption of an older one, is uncertain, but according to the story is commemorative of a strong man. There is a deep notch in the head of it, and the local rhyme tells us that — "Aaron's Knock made this chock." Another stone in the same neighbourhood bears the name of the Blue Jug; it forms a bond-mark to Natsworthy Manor, as also does one called the Grey Wethers Stone. One of the bounds of Blackslade Manor, on the other side of the valley, is known as Grey Goose Nest, and near it is Seven Lords' Lands, a hut circle, where it is said the bounds of seven manors meet. In other parts of the Moor we have, among many others, Old William, Old Jack, Emmet's Post, Handfast, and The Goose. The latter forms one of a line separating Brent Moor from Dean Moor, and the story tells us that it obtains its name in consequence of being mistaken for a goose by a visitor from town who was staying at a farm near by, and had volunteered to go in search of one that was missing. A mist came on while he was on the Moor, and looming up through it he saw what he thought was the bird he was in search of. But only for an instant; for the mist growing more dense obscured every object. To mark the spot he spread his handkerchief on the ground and placed a stone upon it. Luckily he found his way back to the farm, and told what he had done. On the following day, the weather having cleared, he resumed the search, and coming to his mark, found that the supposed goose was only a granite post. He had made sure, he said, on his return, that what he had observed was the missing bird. The farmer replied that he had known better from the first; that in such weather it was impossible for him to have seen a goose unless he had carried a looking-glass with him.

5

Memorials of the Drifts

Horn's Cross, formerly known as Stascombe Telling Place

There is abundant evidence to prove that the men of Devon have exercised their rights upon Darmoor from very early times, and if we hear little about these until that tract of land ceased to be a Royal Forest that is because its recorded history only begins a little over a century previous to that event. Still, it is probable that it was not used before that time to such an extent as afterwards. With disafforestation many restrictions were removed; with the gradual disappearance of the deer there was perhaps an increase in the number of cattle depastured there. But be this as it may, it is certain that for several centuries after it became a Chase in law, which was in 1240, the agistment of cattle upon it received considerable attention, both from its holders, or grantees, and from those who possessed rights of pasturage there, and that the enforcement of the laws regulating this custom formed an important branch of its administration. Officers were appointed to ensure the observance of these laws, and the Moor was carefully searched at certain times, as it is at present, to ascertain whether any cattle had been turned upon it by persons who had no right to do so. These searchings were termed the drifts.

As the Court rolls of the Manor of Lydford contain numerous entries respecting the agistments on the Moor and the gathering of cattle, so on the Moor itself will be found various remains that tell a similar story, The latter are not to be understood, perhaps, by the rambler who is unacquainted with the history of the Moor, but to those who are so they speak, if not eloquently, at least with sufficient clearness. Among other things the documents show us that commoners were frequently presented at the Court for neglecting to keep the hedge, or wall, of the enclosed lands that abutted on the Moor, in a state of repair. When these fences were allowed to fall into a dilapidated condition the cattle were, of course, able to stray from the commons, and much trouble was doubtless occasioned in consequence. We find the same complaint with respect to the gates opening on the Moor, which are often described as ruinous. Fines were levied on persons for leaving the gates open on the days of the drifts, and on venville tenants for not attending the drifts, and bringing with them a man each, as it was their duty to do. Others were presented for turning swine upon the Moor, and for depasturing cattle there without previously entering them on the books of the clerk. One John Somer was so regardless of the custom of the Forest (for Dartmoor though a Chase is usually referred to as a Forest on the court rolls) that he kept a hundred head of cattle on the Moor for a period of five years without licence, and with the result that the bailiff, or forester, was fined for not distraining. John Foger also carried matters with a high hand. He was charged with "daily driving away with his dogs the cattle of divers people agisted in the King's Moor, and making that part of the Moor his own proper common." But, the venville men and commoners of Edward IV, were not to be so disturbed, and Foger was fined for his selfishness. In the time of Henry VIII, as appears from the Receiver-General's account, John Coole and fourteen others were charged at Lydford with having "unlawfully and riotously, in the manner of an insurrection, entered and broke into the liberty of the lord the King of his Manor of Lydford, by commands of the said John Coole, and riotously took and drove away out of the said liberty forty oxen and steers, and ten geldings, of the goods and chattels of the said John Coole, taken by the Bailiff of the lord the King of his Manor aforesaid, and imparked at Brattor within the liberty of the Forest of Dartmoor." John Coole and his associates were, however, more fortunate than John Foger, for as none of the parties dwelt within the liberty of the Forest, and had no goods or chattels there that could be distrained, the amount of the damage, which was laid at a hundred marks, could not be levied.

This, and much of a similar character, do we learn from the Forest records. Now we turn to the Moor for evidences of the drifts of those early days. In several parts of the Forest and commons there are certain spots known to the moormen as Telling-places, and where it is their custom to gather and count the sheep in their charge. There is one on Holne Moor, marked by a broken cross, which is usually known as Stascombe Telling-place, and though its name has been given to it within living memory, it is not unlikely that the old stone was fixed upon as a gathering place for sheep, or cattle, long ago. And that this is so with regard to other similar spots there can be little doubt. Moormen are prone to observe old customs, and can often give you no better reason for doing a thing in a certain way than that they have always done it so, and also their fathers before them. Many of the gates mentioned some three centuries ago are still to be identified, and often the original granite posts remain. There is one at the end of the short lane leading to High Down, near Skit Bridge, which is of more than ordinary interest, as it formed the entrance to the commons from the village of Lydford. Four great slabs are to be seen there, in one being a circular hole, in which the gate swung in the days when iron hinges were unknown on Dartmoor. Below Bellaford Tor, on the path leading from Dunnabridge Pound to Post Bridge, are two or three high granite posts, having notches sunk in them, and which are said to have formed the uprights to which bars were fastened at the time of the drifts.

The Blowing-stone, now in the hedge at Quarry-lane, which leads from Whitchurch Down to the common under Pu Tor, is an interesting memorial of the drifts. When summons to the venville men to attend and their part in searching the Moor was the blast of a horn, the instrument was blown against a stone, hollowed in the manner of a basin, the idea being that the sound would thereby be increased. The horns were blown on the tors near the edge of the Moor.

All the walls on Dartmoor, with the exception of a few of modern date, are very irregularly built, but in some of them what appears to be quite a needless departure from the line in which it is being carried is to be observed. It will suddenly sweep inwards from the common, and roughly describing a semi-circle, will then run on as before. But the builders had a design in this; into the hollow thus formed an animal could be driven and secured. Small enclosures termed courts are also reminiscent of the drifts. There is one of these between Coryndon Ball and Brent Moor. Immediately inside the gate of the latter is a wall running between the Ball and another enclosure, and along by this the Moor road is carried. On the other side of the road is a short piece of wall, and at the end of it a second gate is placed across the road, thus forming a small court. Into this animals are driven from the Moor, and the gates being closed, can be easily secured.

There seems to be some reason for supposing that these courts — or, at all events, courts of this kind — were originally constructed for the purpose of capturing deer. It has been suggested that the "leap-yeats" so frequently mentioned in the court rolls of the Manor and Forest, were not the ordinary Moor "yeats," or gates, but the gates of these small courts, and that the latter were the "leaps." But, however this may be, it is quite certain that they were used for securing cattle at the time of the drifts, and also that some have been built for that purpose since deer have disappeared from the Moor.

The strolls, or strips of common lying between two newtakes, and mostly found near the Moor gates, were partly formed for the purpose of securing cattle. It is true they were also designed for shelters, but the separating of certain beasts from a herd was the chief intention of them. A good example is the long stroll between the Bagga Tor enclosures and those of Longbetor, in the parish of Petertavy. Here the walls, which are not far apart at the Moor gate, gradually recede until quite a large area is formed, and then they once more approach each other. In this space a great number of cattle might be driven, and a couple of horsemen, placed where the walls are not far apart, would be able to prevent their escaping. In nearly every part of the Moor edge strolls may be found, though not always of the size of this one.

When the Forest and commons were searched, all beasts for which owners could not be found were driven to certain pounds on, or near, the Moor. These will be noticed in our next chapter.

6

The Pinfolds

Erme Pound

The cattle pounds existing on Dartmoor, or on its verge, are of two kinds; drift pounds, or those in which estrays, found when the Moor is driven, or searched, are secured; and ordinary parish and manor pounds. Of the former, Dunnabridge Pound, which is situated by the side of the road running from Two Bridges to Dartmeet, is by far the most important, and with the exception of Lough Tor Pound, near by, is the only one within the present bounds of the ancient Royal Forest. It receives frequent mention in various accounts of the Duchy possessions, there being among other matters references to the repairing of the wall and gate, and these go back to the earlier part of the 14th century. But there can be no doubt that Dunnabridge was used as a pound from the times when cattle were first agisted on the Moor. A cursory examination of the wall will be sufficient to convince the investigator that this is built on the foundations of a much older site; that the pound is, in fact, formed on the site of an ancient enclosure of the kind, in which hut circles are often grouped. Lough Tor Pound stands near the tor after which it is named, and is an oblong enclosure, having a high wall, with a wide opening in one of its sides. It is generally regarded as having been used as a sheep pen.

It is probable that at one time Dunnabridge was the only pound to which estrays discovered on the Moor were driven, but later others seem to have come into use. These were Erme Pound, on Harford Moor, in the southern part of Dartmoor, and Creaber Pound, on the verge of Gidleigh Common, in the northern part. But it is likely that the first named was only used in certain cases, whatever may have been the custom with regard to the latter, and that it was to Dunnabridge that animals were eventually taken. Previous to about 1400 the Forest was divided into three bailiwicks, or quarters, only, the north, east, and west. When this arrangement was altered a south quarter was formed, apparently out of the east quarter, and it is not improbable that Erme Pound was thenceforward used at the times of the drifts by the forester of the new bailiwick. Of course, it may have been the custom to drive cattle there from that part of the Forest lying near it prior to that time, but the probability is that when the upper Erme district was included within the east quarter, they were driven direct to Dunnabridge Pound, which was then in the middle of that quarter, and that Erme Pound, which is not in the Forest, was more particularly connected with the venville commons. This point is, however, involved in some obscurity, for not only does the Duchy claim to drive the commons as well as the Forest, but has also exercised other jurisdiction over them. In the Lydford Court rolls, of the time of Henry VIII, mention is made of a piece of land "upon the Common of Devonshire, lying next Erme Pound," having been demised in the preceding reign to Thomas Rawe and others, "to hold according to the custom of the Forest of Dartmoor." It is, therefore quite conceivable that Erme Pound, though not within the Forest, was yet originally a Forest drift pound. Like Dunnabridge, it is formed on the foundations of an ancient enclosure, and several hut circles are to be seen in it.

Creaber Pound is of an entirely different character from any of the other pinfolds on and near the Moor, being, indeed, nothing more than a small down separated from the open common by some farm enclosures. According to a statement made by Sir Thomas Reynell, to whom the Forest was let in the time of Charles I, respecting an estray driven to this pound, it was then the custom to make four drifts for cattle on Dartmoor, one in each of the four quarters of the Forest, at any time between the 23rd June and the 6th August. Animals found in the south, east, and west quarters were driven to Dunnabridge, and those found in the north quarter to Creaber. Any not claimed within three days were driven to Lydford, where there was also a pound, adjoining the castle, where they remained as estrays, and were forfeited if not claimed by the 24th August. This statement was in the form of a bill filed in the Exchequer against Oliver Warren, the owner of the estray in question, a black ox, which not having been claimed, was driven to Lydford. Still remaining unclaimed, it was forfeited to Sir Thomas, its value being appraised at 56s 8d. But Warren brought an action against Sir Thomas's agent, one William Stowel, declaring that after the appraisement at Lydford Castle, the estray ought to have been presented at the following court of the Manor of Lydford and Forest of Dartmoor, within a certain number of days, and declared forfeited by the Duchy steward, but that this was not done, as by the death of the Earl of Pembroke there was no steward, and no court was held. What was the result of this case does not appear, but it is valuable as it stands as showing what was the custom with regard to estrays nearly three hundred years ago, and also that Creaber Pound was in use at that time.

In the court rolls there are numerous references to the "Pinfold of the Castle of Lydford," chiefly concerning its state of repair, and which go to show that the men of Lydford were equally with the inhabitants of other places on and around the Moor, open to the charge of allowing their walls and fences to fall into a dilapidated condition. But they were nevertheless ready enough to make complaint if any damage were done to their pound, as an entry of the 26th of Elizabeth shows. Thomas Standen is charged with having permitted swine to tear up the ground "circa Castr, de Lidford et le Pownd."

On the verge of the common near the gate opening on the enclosed lands belonging to Halstock Farm is Halstock Pound. It is used principally for colts, as the ponies running on the Moor are always termed, and though not now within the bounds of the Forest was certainly so at one time. According to Mr. W. Burt in his Preface to Carrington's "Dartmoor," it was the custom to make an additional drive in the east quarter of the Forest for colts, but whether these were driven to Halstock, which is in Okehampton parish, and on the borders of the north quarter, does not appear. At a court of survey held at Lydford Castle, in 1786, forty years before Mr. Burt wrote, the jurors state that it was the custom to make, in addition to three drifts for cattle, which were commonly called summer drifts, one winter drift for colts, and that these were to be driven to Dunnabridge Pound, and thence, after "two days and three nights," to Lydford to the Prince's Pound. The jurors do not mention Halstock Pound. The pound is a small one, of a square shape, the wall being well built. It was probably mostly used as a manor pound.

It does not appear that there was ever any drift pound on the western side of Dartmoor. In more recent times estrays found in that part of the west quarter, or on the commons, in the neighbourhood of Mis Tor, have often been driven in the first instance to Merivale Bridge, and temporarily secured in a newtake there, and it is not unlikely that such a course was followed from the time land was first enclosed there. Burt states that Grim's Pound, the ancient hut enclosure in the east part of the Moor, was for some time used for confining estrays, but it is more probable that, like Merivale, it merely served the purpose of a gathering-place for cattle, and that animals were only kept there a little while before being driven to Dunnabridge.

Among the parish and manor pounds found on the borders of the Moor, the one at Belstone is remarkable for its unusual shape, which is circular. We can well imagine that in days gone by this pound fully justified its existence. The Belstone men have always been great upholders of their rights, and there can be little doubt that any animals found straying within the bounds of their parish were speedily driven to the pinfold. The tiny manor pound at Gidleigh may also be deemed remarkable by some, not, indeed, as being circular, but as presenting no shape at all, or, to be more correct, one that cannot well be described. But belonging as it does to a manor the lords of which were the possessors of one of the few castles existing on the borders of Dartmoor, it is endowed with a particular interest.

In the parish of Widecombe, and on the brow of the hill, overlooking the beautiful Holne Chase, is the hamlet of Pound's Gate. This, in all probability, derives its name from the pound still to be seen there. It is situated by the side of the road near one of the entrances to Spitchwick, and is rectangular in shape, with a well-built wall. Close to it is a gate opening on a kind of stroll now leading to a field.

Mention is made on the court rolls of Lydford of the 18th Edward IV, of a pound that seems to have been situated near the Torry, the tributary of the Plym that rises under Pen Beacon and falls into that river at Long Bridge. John Hawston, of Elburton, is stated to have been in the habit of yearly driving much of the southern part of Dartmoor, and impounding the cattle there agisted in the pinfold at Torrycombe. The valley of the Torry below Tolch Moor Bridge is still known by this name.

In the little village of Shaugh is a small pound, of very rude construction, and now in a ruinous condition. It is not far from the White Thorn Inn, and on the right of the way in approaching the village from the bridge. One side of it is formed by a hedge, the others being constructed of blocks of granite; the entrance is at the end. At Meavy there is also a small square pound, but of a different character. Here the wall is of masonry, but the place, having been long disused, is overgrown with vegetation. It stands by the side of the road leading to Marchants Bridge.

At Cudlipptown, in the parish of Petertavy, is a manor pound, very similar in style to that at Meavy, but in a better state of preservation. It is now unused, and weeds and briars cover the space in which formerly many a straying animal stood and looked wistfully through the bars of the gate at the few chance passers-by, or gazed longingly at the sweet grass it prevented him from reaching. Another pound in this parish is perhaps as interesting as any in the Dartmoor borderland. It is the ancient pinfold at Willsworthy, a manor that includes within its bounds a large tract of Moor. Situated close to the Willsworthy Brook, where that stream is crossed by a clapper (though now modernised), and where formerly stood an ancient chapel that served the needs of the settlers in the Tavy, and in the midst of the semi-wild scenery characteristic of the verge of the great waste, this memorial of old times cannot but interest the visitor. Its rude wall is formed of large granite blocks, between which moss and tiny ferns are growing; two large stones, one of them declining from its once upright position, mark the entrance to this little pound.

At Horndon, in the adjoining parish of Marytavy, there is also a pound, or, perhaps it would be more correct to say, the remains of one. This part of the moorlands was evidently colonised by farm settlers who pushed their way up the valley of the Tavy, and there is still much to remind the visitor of the customs of an older day. Among these memorials the now disused pounds will not be the least striking.

35

7

Guide-stones

Bennet's Cross

We have already seen that the principal tracks in the southern and western parts of Dartmoor were those by means of which communication was kept up between the abbeys on the borders of the waste, and which were marked in places by rude granite crosses. It has also been observed that there were other paths, used by the Forest dwellers, and these there can be no doubt were of even earlier date than the monks' paths. The Lich Path which leads from the settled part of the East Dart valley to Lydford, and the Church Way, running over the southern end of the Hameldon ridge to Widecombe, it is not unlikely are coeval with the earliest of the farm settlements in the Forest, while Cut Lane, which crosses the hill of fen between the valleys of the East Dart and the Upper Tavy, or Amicombe, is in all probability yet more ancient. Another path that ran across the Forest is also of considerable antiquity, though we cannot be sure that it dates back to so early a period as the others we have named. But while the Lich Path and Cut Lane in the course of time were to fall into comparative disuse, this track was to become the most important on Dartmoor. The former are now grass-grown, and in places cannot be traced; the latter is a broad highway, and forms the most direct road from Plymouth to Exeter.

With few exceptions the ancient tracks that are still to be seen on the Moor are merely green paths, traversed only by the Moorman or the hunter. And it is certain that they were never anything more than this, for even when in use by the Forest men the traffic over them could not have been great. There was no attempt at making a road; the way was worn by the hoofs of Moor ponies, or, as in the case of the Abbots' Way, by the monks' palfreys and the pack-horse of the yarn-jobber. The most frequented, no doubt, became clearly defined in certain places, but where the nature of the ground did not necessitate a certain line being strictly followed; the track would often be lost. On the monks' paths the cross would point the way in such spots; on the others it was usual to erect guide-stones, and many of these still exist on the Moor.

The precursor of the Plymouth and Exeter highway may not have come into existence until long after the rude enclosures of Saxon times were formed in the Forest, but it is nevertheless certain that many centuries have elapsed since first the way was traversed. It is true that until the closing years of the eighteenth century, when modern roads were first made on Dartmoor, there was very little traffic over it; but as by this track the distance between the two towns named would be shorter than the route to the north or south of the Moor by many miles, we cannot doubt that it was always in use, if only to a small extent. The objections that travellers might have to passing through such a desolate region, as Dartmoor was a century and a half ago, would be partly removed by the considerations that this particular track lay through that part of it in which the Forest farms were situated. The former existence of crosses on this road, to be presently noticed, may be taken as a proof of its use in early times, and though these do not show it to have been a monks' path, like those leading to and from the Abbeys, there is yet little doubt that it formed the way by which the good brothers of Tavistock and Buckland journeyed to the eastern side of the Moor.

That this road was formerly marked by guide-stones is proved by an entry in the Municipal Records of Plymouth, which sets forth under the date 1699—1700 that a sum of £2 was paid towards defraying the expenses of setting up stones on Dartmoor, on the road leading from the town to Exeter, for the purpose of guiding travellers; and that the Rundle Stone, which stood on a branch of this road, leading to Tavistock, was also in existence at, or about that time, is shown by its mention, as we have already stated, in 1702. The situation of this stone on the Forest boundary line shows it to have been a bond mark, but that it served as a guide-stone as well there is evidence to prove. The Exeter road enters the Moor at Peak Hill, not far from Dousland, and is carried over the shoulder of that eminence. On its northern side, and on the left of the way in going to Princetown, is a stone, which may not improbably be one of those erected some two centuries ago by the Plymouth Corporation. It is known as Goad's Stone, and marks a point where a green track, coming up from Walkhampton, joins the highway. It is of small size, and is usually regarded being an old milestone; some faint markings may be traced upon it, but whether they are artificial is doubtful.

The section of this road between Chagford and Two Bridges is shown on a plan in Owen's edition of Ogilby's survey of the principal roads in England and Wales, entitled "Britannia Depicta," the continuation of it, from Two Bridges to Tavistock, being also shown. This book appeared in 1720, but when Ogilby made his survey I am unable to say. The road entered the Moor near Metherall Farm, and a stone which may still be seen there probably marked its direction. Some two miles further on the words "Heath Stone" occur, the stone itself being figured, and near it the road was joined by one coming from Moretonhampstead. This object, like the Rundle Stone, also receives mention in 1702, as does the ancient Bennet's Cross, which yet stands on the common not far off. Another old cross, which formerly stood on Meripit Hill, and was seen there by the Rev. E. A. Bray in 1831, is shown on the plan as "a stone called Merry Pit," and further on, after passing the West Dart, the Rundle Stone is figured, and marked "Great Stone call'd Roundle."

Many years ago I learnt from Jonas Coaker, formerly well known in the neighbourhood as the Dartmoor poet, that a cross once stood by the side of this road near the entrance to Standon, in the hamlet of Post Bridge, and which he said was known as Maggie Cross. He remembered it, but was unable to say what had become of it. There were thus three crosses on the moorland section of the Plymouth and Exeter road, besides guide-stones, the latter probably being not far apart, if we may judge from what may be seen in other localities. On that part of the road between Moor Gate and Moreton, a distance of four miles, two of these will be found, one at Beetor Cross and another about a mile from the town. On them are inscribed the initial letters of the places to which roads lead from the spots on which they stand.

A row of guide-stones may be seen on Long Ash Hill, above Merivale Bridge, which formerly marked the way leading from Tavistock to Ashburton, as the letters cut upon them indicate. This road crossed the Walkham below the present Merivale Bridge at a ford, and was really a part of the Tavistock branch of the old Abbots' Way, but whether the guide-stones were set up before the erection of a bridge at Merivale is doubtful. The track seems to have crossed over the southern shoulder of North Hisworthy, and to have passed near where Princetown now stands, from which point it apparently went on to Childe's Tomb. Here the path now known as Sandy Way formed its continuation to Holne Moor. Near the source of the Wennaford Brook it probably left Sandy Way, and ran to Holne Moor Gate, the present road to Ringleshutts Mine, it is not unlikely, being formed upon it. At the point where this mine road leaves the Holne and Hexworthy road a guide-stone may still be seen.

On White Ridge, between Post Bridge and Teign Head, there is a path marked by guide-stones, but these are of comparatively recent erection. They were set up by a miner some thirty or forty years ago who was in the habit of passing over the hill from his house at Standon to Knock Mine, on the Taw, where he was employed.

Although I have made search, I have been unable to discover any guide-stones on the King Way, the old path which ran along the northern verge of the Moor from Tavistock to Okehampton, further than the slab, cut into the form of a cross, which now forms the seventh milestone from the first-named town. But, as much of the track has been obliterated by modern roads, and encroachments on the commons, it is only to be expected that any stones of this kind that may have existed would be removed or broken up. There are, however, several objects on this path that may have served as marks to it, such as cairns, and natural rocks, and in one place there is a row of granite posts. These, however, are really bond stones, and mark a point where Okehampton Common runs up into Sourton Common, and which is known as Iron Gates. Here a space much wider than usual is left between two of the stones in this row, and shows where the King Way passed.

These instances of boundary stones also serving as guide-stones are not uncommon. There is one at Dick's Well, at the head of the Doe Tor Brook. A stone pillar is there placed to mark the boundary of the common lands belonging to the parishes of Sourton and Lydford, but it is also useful as a guide to a peat track running out to the Forest. Ancient crosses also serve both as boundary marks and guide-stones, and in more than one instance menhirs are put to these purposes. There is some reason for believing the pillar known as Bear Down Man to be a guide-stone rather than a menhir, though we shall probably be nearer the mark if we suppose it to be a genuine example of the latter adopted in very early times as a mark to a way across the Moor.

Sometimes paths are found marked by little mounds instead of erect stones, as in the case of the green track leading from Owley to Harford. The track in Cut Combe is marked in this manner, but there the mounds are surmounted by upright stones. The two large slabs on this path, placed where the fen has been removed, are probably the most ancient guide-stones in the Forest.

Among other stones that marked paths traversed by the wayfarer in past days may be mentioned several on the southern edge of the Moor, on which the names of towns are indicated by their initial letters; also the pillar known as Emmett's Post, on Shaugh Common; and Forstal, or Fostal, Cross, a pillar on the Lich Path. This stands on Black Down, near the Redford enclosures, at a point where the ancient track named is crossed by another running from Brent Tor to the Forest. Locally it is often called Postal Cross.

Other guide-stones will be found marking the paths leading to warrens, and these are mostly of comparatively modern date. Some may be seen on Ringmoor Down, on the track running out to Ditsworthy Warren, and others on the side of Pupers, between the in-country near Hayford and Huntingdon Warren. One of these, which stands near a reave extending from the summit of Pupers to Water Oke Corner, is known as Kit's Stone. Kit, who worked at Huntingdon Mine, was returning home one evening, after having made an incursion into the Warren, in the absence of its owner, when on reaching this stone he was met by that individual. The warrener, noticing his pockets, at once divined what had occurred. He, however, said nothing but began pitying Kit's poverty, and expressed himself at being sorry that he had no better clothes than the rags he was wearing. At length he vowed Kit should have his coat, which was a good one, and said that he would make shift with the miner's. Kit, who saw the warrener's drift, pretended to be very reluctant to deprive him of his garment, but while talking, contrived to push the rabbits which he had in his pockets, through the torn lining, inside the waist-band of his capacious corduroy breeches. Then pretending to yield, he took off his coat, but would not give it up until the warrener had handed his over to him. Having received it, Kit put it on, and quietly walked off. The next morning the warrener approached him, while at his work. "I was deceived last night," he said; "I ought not to have changed coats." "Aw, ees, that was all right," replied Kit, "if you'd aunly a volley'd it up. You auft to ha' changed another garment too."

8

Spanning the Torrents

The clapper at Postbridge

The streams of Dartmoor when flooded by the melting of winter snows, or by heavy rains in summer, become formidable obstacles to progress, and on this account we find that the ancient tracks were often carried near their heads where the freshets would be least likely to render them impassable. But this, of course, could not always be done, and bridges therefore became necessary in places. These were not arched structures, but were formed of immense slabs of granite laid upon rudely-built piers and buttresses, and are always known on the Moor as clappers.

An idea was formerly prevalent that these bridges belonged to pre-historic times, and that the ringing of the chariot wheels of the Damnonian warrior upon the huge stones might once have been heard above the roar of the waters. Indeed, this romantic notion has apparently not yet altogether died out. Only last year an article appeared in a London daily from the pen of a well-known author in which it found a place. It is true that his description of his walk over Dartmoor showed him to have very little acquaintance with it, and this may probably be the reason for writing as he did. It would also be a sufficient reason why he should not have written on Dartmoor at all.

It was no doubt the uncommon appearance of these bridges that led to the belief that they were of very early date. The roadway of flat stones resting on roughly-built piers, no mortar being used, rendered them totally unlike anything seen elsewhere, and it was consequently supposed that they were erected at a time when the arch was unknown here. Composed of massive blocks, which it must have required considerable skill to place in position, they were referred to some half-century ago as cyclopean bridges, and were connected in the minds of antiquaries with the stone remains on the Moor. But that the days which saw the erection of the oldest of them would not take us far back into the history of the Moor is certain, while others, though now presenting an appearance that may not inaptly be described as venerable, cannot boast of an age greater than a couple of centuries, and some are even of a day still nearer to our own. The earliest, there is not doubt, were built by the farm settlers on the Moor, and from that time they have continued to be constructed. Dartmoor abounds with scattered granite, and wherever a bridge was required, there the necessary material was to be found. Clappers may be seen in every part of the borderland of Dartmoor, but the finest examples are found on the tracks leading to the ancient Forest tenements.

The earliest mention of a bridge on Dartmoor, so far as I can discover, occurs in the charter of Isabella de Fortibus, Countess of Albemarle and Devon, confirming the grant of lands by her mother to Buckland Abbey, and which was signed at Brommon in 1291. There the precursor of the present Cadaford Bridge on the Plym is named. This appears in the document as the "ponte de Cadaworth," and that it was a clapper similar to those now existing is very probable. But while this seems to be the earliest reference to a Dartmoor bridge, there is one to a crossing-place over a Dartmoor stream two hundred and sixty years earlier. In 1031 Cnut granted to one of his thegns, named Ætheric, half a "mansa" of land at Mœwi, or Meavy, as is set forth in a charter in the King's Library in the British Musuem, and which is also to be found in Kemble. The boundaries are given, and commence in the north-east corner of the parish at a point named the "Cleaca." The late Mr. James B. Davidson, well-known as an Anglo-Saxon scholar, being struck with this phrase, visited the spot in order to ascertain, if possible, the meaning of it, and communicated the result of his investigations to "The Academy" in 1882. At the spot indicated he found a set of stepping-stones, and unhesitatingly identified these with the object named in the charter. The name he considered to be a survival, through the Anglo-Saxon period, of the Celtic "clachran," or "clachan," the former being explained in Armstrong's Celtic Dictionary as "a pier, landing-place, stepping-stones in water or on watery ground," and the latter being rendered in O'Reilly's Irish-English Dictionary "a ford, stepping-stones." It seems to me not improbable that "clapper" may have been derived from the Saxon form of this word.

42

The largest and most striking of the Dartmoor clappers is Post Bridge, on the East Dart, and this being situated close to the principal road across the Moor, is also the best known. I have heard the tracks on the Moor sometimes spoken of by the natives as "old post roads," and it is likely that this bridge derived its name in that connection, and in turn gave it to the hamlet that has sprung up near it. In Owen's "Britannia Depicta" (referred to in Chapter VII), published in 1720, it appears on the plan as "Post Stone Bridge, 3 arches," the latter word, of course, referring to the openings. The present county bridge, which spans the river just above the old structure, has three arches, but this was not built until after 1772, in which year the Act for making the first road over Dartmoor was obtained. I have known those whose parents recollected when the clapper afforded the only means of crossing the Dart at this point when it was in flood. The stones of which these bridges are built are almost entirely in their natural state, little having been done to them except a rough working of their surfaces in order to make them bear firmly, and the shaping of those forming the upper end of the piers in such a manner as to give the latter an angular form, and thus offer the least resistance to the water. The length of the clapper at Post Bridge is nearly forty-three feet, and its height from the bed of the river in the centre eight and a half feet. It is not, however, quite so high as this throughout, as the roadway is not flat, but slightly arched. This latter is formed by four slabs, one being placed across the western opening, another across the eastern, and two spanning the centre waterway. The former are rather more than fifteen feet in length; the other two are over twelve feet. At its narrowest part the bridge is about six and a half feet in width. One of the centre stones was intentionally thrown off many years ago, and lay for some time in the bed of the river. Unfortunately when it was replaced it was not put into its original position, what was its upper face now being its under one, and its ends being reversed.

Further down the Dart are the remains of another fine clapper, now replaced, like Post Bridge, by a modern erection. This is situated near Bellaford Farm, and appears to be referred to in the Lydford Court Rolls of the 7th of James I. Still further down, at Dartmeet, are the buttresses of another, destroyed by a flood in 1826, and which was partly rebuilt some years ago. Between these two points a stream called the Walla Brook falls into the Dart, and not far above the confluence is spanned by a clapper in an excellent state of preservation. It is about twenty-three feet in length, and though not very wide, is sufficiently so to permit of the passing of a pack-horse.

It is rather strange that no remains of a clapper are found in the West Dart in the neighbourhood of Hexworthy, seeing that Forest tenements existed there on both banks of the river, and this, I think, can only be accounted for on the supposition that such a structure was destroyed when the present modern bridge was built there. There is no clapper now to be seen on any part of the West Dart, although it is certain that one must have existed near where the hamlet of Two Bridges now stands. On the plan in the "Britannia Depicta" the track across the Forest is shown as running by which is marked as "A rocky hill call'd Crockhan Tor," and not far from this, where the road crosses a stream, are the words "Dart Flue, Stone Bridge." This is evidently the point where the modern county bridge was afterwards built, and close to which the hamlet of Two Bridges came into existence, though whether the older structure crossed the Dart below the confluence with the Cowsic, as the present bridge does, or above it, is not certain. There is some reason for believing that the latter was the case. It is also known that another clapper spanned the Dart a short distance below the hamlet. In a charming dell below Bear Down Farm, and not far above where the Cowsic mingles its waters with the larger stream, is a most interesting example of a clapper. The piers are small, and the roadway is not carried very high above the water, but the bridge is of considerable length.

In 1831 the Rev. E. A. Bray, of Tavistock, visited Dunnabridge, on the West Dart, for the purpose of discovering, if possible, a stone said to have been removed from Crockern Tor. He was surprised at finding no bridge there, thinking that the name of the place was derived from such an object. But the derivation is probably to be found in the ancient drift found there, or in a circular enclosure near to it, both, there is little doubt, the sites of ancient settlements. It is highly probable that "bridge," is merely a corruption of "brig," or "brug," indeed, both these forms occur in early documents relating to the Forest. In an account of the profits of the Moor, in 1304, the name appears as Donebrugge, and in another of about fifty years later, as Donabrigge. It is not unlikely that in the name of this old pound we see the Celtic "dun," a hill, and "brug," a village, that is, the hill settlement, a term which there is no doubt once well described it. At all events, no bridge exists near there, nor are the traces of any to be found. The small bridge over the stream near the pound, it may be explained, is of quite recent erection, and does not replace any ancient structure.

Two clappers are to be seen near Princetown, one at the Ockery, on the Blackabrook, and the other at Fitz's Well, further up the same stream. Low parapets have been added to the former, but otherwise it is still in its primitive state. The clapper near the well has been rebuilt; it was partly swept away during a flood in 1873. Another good example in the neighbourhood will be found close to Long Ash Farm, near Merivale.

Other rude bridges of this description may be seen on the Bagga Tor Brook and Willsworthy Brook, both tributaries of the Tavy; at Hall Farm, on the verge of Black Down; at the head of the Lyd; under East Mil Tor, spanning the Blackaven; on the Taw, above the narrow gorge on the western side of Steeperton Tor; below the solitary farmhouse near the source of the Teign; at Runnage and Pizwell, on the Walla Brook; at Shallowford, on the West Webburn; at Leighon, on the Becky Brook; in the valley of Widecombe; at Huntingdon, Trowlesworthy, under Lether Tor, and other parts of the Moor. These belong to different periods, some being of a very primitive type, but they are all of one general character.

Among single stone clappers examples are to be found at Fernworthy, in the east part of the Forest; on the Walla Brook, in the same neighbourhood, close to which, on the Teign, are the vestiges of a bridge referred to two centuries ago as Ting Clapper; at Cross Furzes, on the verge of Dean Moor,

44

where the stone bears the dates 1705 and 1737; and at Harford, near Ivybridge. A good one also exists at Halstock, near Okehampton, but can no longer be seen, as the road having been raised it is buried beneath the soil.

On the borders of the Moor wooden bridges are sometimes found, and are known as clams. These, however, are comparatively rare on Dartmoor, as might be expected in a district where stone is as abundant as wood is scarce.

The old clappers of our Devonshire uplands are not only interesting in themselves, but also appeal to us as links between the present and the earlier days of the Forest settlers. Some few have perhaps been swept away by angry floods, and some have been thoughtlessly destroyed. But as the light spreads there will be greater reverence for that which is old, and we may hope that henceforth the vandal's hand will not be raised against them. We will hope, too, that the waters may spare them; that no link in the chain shall be broken.

9

The Toilers by the Streams

Remains of Crazing Mill at Gobbett Mine

Having in previous articles given some account of the ancient Stannary laws, by which the tin mining in Devon was regulated, we now propose to offer a few remarks on the objects found in and near the stream works on the Moor. It is impossible to ramble through any of the river valleys there without meeting with examples of these. On the banks of every principal stream, and tributary brooks of any importance, heaps of stones thrown up by the men who delved here for ore may be seen, and these are sometimes scattered over an extensive area. In no case do they deface the Moor, for the stones are weathered, and covered with short, grey moss, and between them tiny ferns are often growing. Among these heaps will sometimes be found the ruins of small buildings, and lying near them large blocks of granite, in which are the hollows that served as mortars, and the moulds into which the smelted tin was poured.

Dwarf walls are often met with, and wheel pits, and partly filled-up watercourses and other evidences of the tinners' industry. In these workings tin was only sought for on the surface. The gravels containing the ore were placed on an inclined plane, and while this was agitated a stream of water was directed over it, and the gravel was thus separated from the tin. This process was known as streaming.

Into the question of the age of these workings we do not now propose to enter, but nothing is more certain than that tin was sought for on Dartmoor at a very early time. But it is also equally certain that streaming was continued there until a comparatively recent period, and it is therefore probable that the traces of most of the more ancient workings have been obliterated by the miners of later days, who, it is very likely, often chose them as the scene of their own ventures. Down to the time of Queen Elizabeth, tin mining was an important industry on Dartmoor, though it appears to have declined somewhat during the years immediately preceding her reign, and we shall, therefore, probably not be wrong if we regard the greater number of the objects found in the stream works as belonging to a period antecedent to her time. One of those tin works is mentioned by name as early as 1240. In the Perambulation of the Forest made in that year we find the line drawn by the perambulators from the stream now known as the Wobrook to "la Dryework." This object is also named as a bound by the Jury of Survey, who made a return of the boundaries in 1609. They set forth the line as running up the Wobrook to "Drylake, alias Dryewoorke." Today the spot is known as Drylakes, and consists of an extensive stream work. Mention is also made in the first Perambulation of what was probably a place for the smelting of ore, though apart from its name there is nothing to enable us now to identify it as such. This is a bound called King's Oven, and is situated about a quarter of a mile northward of the Warren House Inn, on the Princetown and Moreton road. It is merely a circular enclosure with a few worked stones in its centre. But we hear of the tinners in connection with Dartmoor before the date of the Perambulation. In 1216 the custodian of Lydford Castle is commanded to permit the "men of Joan, Queen of England," to take peat from Dartmoor for use in the Stannary, and 1222 it is ordered that the "tinners of Devon" should be allowed to supply themselves with fuel "in our Moor of Dartmoor."

The working tinners were known as spalliards, "with whom," says Risdon, "there is no labourer in hardness of life to be compared," and it is at the scenes where these men delved that we shall now briefly glance, in order that we may discover what they have left behind to tell of the manner of their working.

Not far from Princetown the Mew flows below the rocks of Black Tor, and here in a charming little dell, where the stream tumbles suddenly over some grey boulders into a fern-fringed pool, are the ruins of two small buildings, the nature of which is clearly indicated by the extensive stream work at the head of which they stand. One is placed on the left bank of the Mew, and the other on the right bank. The former is about twenty-two feet in length, and sixteen in width, and has a very perfect entrance. On one side of it is a wheel-pit, the wall of which is composed of very large blocks of granite. The other building is not in such a good state of preservation, and is much smaller, but nevertheless possesses one or two interesting features. A portion of the chimney is still standing, and there are also a couple of stones with the circular hollows in them in which the tin was pounded. Further down the Mew, near Lether Tor Bridge, there are also some curious stones which were evidently connected with mining, and the whole neighbourhood has been very industriously worked.

Those houses in which the tin was smelted were known as blowing-houses, and we learn that it was a practice of the tinners to set fire to them at times in order to recover the particles of tin which had lodged in the thatched roof. As an old chronicler humorously remarks, it is not often that we hear of a profit being made by the deliberate destruction of property.

The bank of the Tavy between Ger Tor and the fine group of rocks usually known as the Tavy Cleave Tors has been streamed, and further up the same river, near where it receives the Rattle Brook, there is also an extensive working. Here above the left bank, on the side of a hill called Knowle, is a large mound which goes by the name of the Lord Mayor's Castle. It does not appear to be a tumulus of the ordinary kind, and being in such close proximity to the stone heaps of the tinners it is not unlikely that it was thrown up by them. There is another mound of a similar kind above the bank of the Rattle Brook, not far distant, which also seems to have been connected with some workings. Opposite to the Lord Mayor's Castle is a fine group of hut circles, and among these is a little building which, though it certainly does not appear to belong to the same period as they do, can hardly be identified as an erection of the tinners. It is something in the nature of a recess, and is built against the hill. If not connected with the mining remains nearby, it was possibly a shepherd's shelter. Above the working is Red Lake Combe, in which, if it be the same as is referred to in the Court rolls of Lydford in the time of James I, there was formerly a "clashmill." The entry refers to a surrender of land together with this mill, "in Redlakecombe, in the west part of Dartmore."

It is sometimes possible to identify these mills, as they are termed in the Foresters' accounts, with existing remains. A sum of 3d, is returned as rent for "a mill called Wallack Mill," in 1538 or 1539, which there is good reason to believe refers to a ruin on the Black Lane Brook, in the south quarter. There is also mention at the same time of another mill called Kakkling Mill, but of the identity of this we cannot be quite so sure. Above the bank of the Erme is a shallow combe known to the Moormen as Knocking Mill, and many years ago I discovered there some traces of mining buildings, and it is possible that the entry may have reference to these. There is a blowing-house at the foot of Stony Bottom, on the Erme, where is a very large tin-work. This is referred to in an 18th century document, in which the bounds are entered, but as a work already in existence, and there can be no doubt whatever that it is of very much earlier date. The house is twenty-seven feet in length, and more than seventeen feet in width. Immediately within the entrance is a large stone, in which is a mould one foot long, and about three and a half inches wide. The sides of it are sloping, so as to permit of the ready removal of the ingot. It is between three and four inches deep. In some instances a tiny mound is found close to the larger one. This is supposed to have been intended for the casting of miniature ingots as samples.

Some good examples of mould stones may be seen in two blowing-houses near the source of the Yealm. Here we find a mould nearly a foot and a half in length and about a foot wide, and eight inches in depth, and several others also of large size. One of these houses is situated on the eastern bank, and the other, which is nearly a quarter of a mile further up the stream, on the western bank. The former is in a very ruinous state, but the latter is a fair example of these erections. In many of these blowing-houses the remains of the fireplaces are to be seen, and a recess is not infrequently found in them. Usually the entrance is near the corner in one of the longer sides.

The remains of a crazing mill formerly at Gobbett, near Hexworthy, were particularly interesting as an example of the ancient mode of grinding the ore either by hand or by horse power. Other remains near Hexworthy are to be seen near the confluence of the West Dart and the Wobrook. Here is a building locally known as the Mill, in which are some good examples of mortar-stones. At Deep Swincombe, in the same neighbourhood, is a trough, hollowed out of a rock, which, from its proximity to a blowing-house, was doubtless made and used by the miners. In the locality the building is always known as the Pigs' House, the trough placed in front of it conveying to the peasantry this idea of its use. What the purpose of the trough was is not quite clear; its size will hardly permit us to regard it as a mould. Similar troughs, not, however, cut in the rocks, are found in and near many of the stream works.

It will sometimes be seen that the river near a tin work is confined within walls, as though for the purpose of damming back the water. Such an arrangement may be noticed on the Brock Hill stream, in the south part of the Moor, and on the Steeperton Brook in the north; also on the Walla Brook, where it falls into the North Teign, and on the East Dart. On the latter stream quite a long stretch is confined between walls, these being formed by granite blocks rudely shaped. Apparently this was done for the purpose of ponding back the water in order to ensure a continuous supply for the Vitifer Mine leat, this being taken from the Dart, near the lower end of the walls, where hatches were probably once fixed. Above this walled-in part of the river is the extensive stream work at Broad Marsh.

At Vitifer are some ancient shafts, which, circular in form, and cased with stones, much resemble wells. In this part of the Moor mining still flourishes.

The ruined buildings and stone heaps, the hollowed granite boulders and troughs, the water-courses, and deep pits, are not all that the "old men," as the Dartmoor native calls the tinners, have left upon the Moor. There are other objects that we may see, and to enable us the better to do so we will take one of these ancient miners for our guide, and with him visit some of the workings among the hills.

10

Some Haunts of the "Old Men"

Arme Pits

On the 20th day of September, 1758, the bounds of a tin-work at Huntingdon, in the south quarter of the Forest of Dartmoor, and within the Stannary of Ashburton, were cut and pitched by Sampson German. There is little doubt that Sampson was full of hope when he undertook this work; had excellent reasons, or thought he had, for believing that it would be profitable; that a goodly quantity of tin would be obtained. Whether his expectations were realised of course we cannot know, but judging from the numerous heaps of debris that are to be seen on the site marked out by him, besides indications of the smelting of ore, it would certainly appear that he or his successors were not disappointed in their search. It may not be altogether uninteresting if we carry our imagination back to that September day, nigh upon a century and a half ago, when Sampson went to Huntingdon to take the first step in his venture.

We will go there too and make his acquaintance. It may fall out that he will have something to tell us concerning the miners and their work.

As we approach the hill, round which the Avon flows to meet the Wellabrook, we see the worthy adventurer, with some companions, apparently engaged in cutting turf. We are welcomed, and speedily learn that Sampson is setting out his tin bounds. The manner of doing this, he explains, is first to make four corner-bounds, two at the head of the work and two at the foot, or, as he terms it, the tail. Then between these are placed head-bounds and side-bounds, all being made by cutting three slabs of turf and standing them on their edges in the form of a triangle. The marks on one side must be opposite to those on the other, and the bounds must be renewed once a year. Sometimes, so we learn, stones may take the place of turf, and Sampson also tells us of the little heaps called stannaburrows that the miners throw up as bondmarks.

Having finished his cutting and pitching, the worthy adventurer speaks of other stream works in the locality, and mentions some curious pits at the head of the Erme. On learning that we should like to see them, he readily agrees to accompany us thither, and we set out together to climb the hill on the further side of the Avon. Sampson calls it the Aune, and we notice, too, that his pronunciation of the name of the river to the source of which we are going is not that which the usual form of spelling would lead us to suppose. Indeed, when he mentioned the workings there we imagined that he was talking about something very different, until we discovered that by armpits he meant, not the axillae, but pits on the Arme. After crossing the river Sampson leads the way up the steep hillside, taking us along the edge of a narrow gully, which, as he tells us, is called Piper's Beam. The latter term, he says, is found in different parts of the Moor, and always in connection with similar gullies, or gerts, as they are often called, excavated by the miners, and he therefore takes it to mean an open working. He mentions among others Higher Liners Beam, Gibby's Beam, and Cater's Beam, the last name having also attached itself to a hill near the working on which it was first bestowed. Sampson then takes us down to Red Lake, and shows us how it has been streamed throughout its course, the heaps of stones thrown up by the "old men," extending from the point where it leaves the mire in which it rises to its union with the Erme. We pass over Green Hill to the Black Lane Brook, where there is a very large working, the head of it being near to a branch of that stream flowing from a great depression on the fen called Ducks' Pool, which was probably once filled with water. We halt by the side of a small building, at one end of which is a fireplace, while our guide explains to us that on the further side of the extensive tract of fen near Fox Tor, and also towards Aune Head, similar tin-works are to be seen. Then as we make our way downward among the stone heaps he bids us notice the manner in which they were piled. This has been done with great regularity, and we notice that each heap is retained within a dry wall. Sampson tells us that this mode of piling the stones is by no means uncommon, but that in the present instance much more care than is usual has been bestowed upon the work. Further down the stream we come upon two more buildings, of a similar oblong shape to the other, but larger; then, leaving the great grey heaps, we pass through a rocky hollow, and mounting the slope above the right bank, soon after find ourselves, as Sampson says, at Arme Pits. These excavations extend for some little distance down the hill, but Sampson tells us that beyond the source of the Arme there are others, larger and deeper. To these he accordingly leads the way, and presently we find ourselves on the verge of one of them, in the midst of broken ground, and scattered rocks, and heaps of stone. This pit is, as our guide has said, of considerable size, as also is another that adjoins it. In each is one of the little oblong buildings like those we have already met with, and which, indeed, are found in nearly every stream-work on the Moor. While we are examining them Sampson tells us that these workings have long been famous for yielding abundance of tin. Formerly, he says, a particular kind of ore called zill tin was obtained here. It was like grit, or small sand, and not only needed nothing but washing, but could be smelted more easily than any other sort of tin ore. About a hundred years since (previous to 1670), he goes on to say, one, Thomas Creber, of Plympton St. Mary, laboured here, and at Eylesbarrow, in the Plym Valley, as indeed had his ancestors, and was a man, so he had heard, well skilled in all that pertained to the mining of tin.

Leaving these deep pits, not without being impressed by the magnitude of the operations of the "old men" in this part of the Moor, we follow our guide through the wilderness of stones immediately below the source of the Erme, and reaching the left bank of the stream, follow it downward. Crossing Red Lake we draw near to Erme Pound, where close to the entrance Sampson shows us a curious little building, having a low stone bench running round its interior. Though similar in size and shape to the houses of the miners, Sampson tells us that he thinks it may have been built as a shelter for those who gathered at the pound at such times as cattle were driven to it; at all events, he says, it is always used by those who attend the drifts. They make merry there, too, we learn, and as proof of this our guide points to the numerous fragments of stone jars that lie around. Not far from it is another building, which, he thinks, was also erected for the accommodation of the herdsmen and commoners, and which, like the former, is crowded on drift days. But if these be not miners' houses there are yet many in the valley, and some of them in use, too, as he will presently show us, and so we set off once more.

Sampson takes us to the foot of Stony Bottom, where Hook Lake joins the Erme. Here men are working, and we see the smelted tin being poured into the mould cut in the granite block. The stream-work extends to the head of the tributary, the clouded waters of which bring down large quantities of sand. All along its banks tinners are busily employed, some digging, others adding to the stone heaps, and others again washing the ore. After having looked awhile upon the scene, Sampson German bids us follow him, and choosing a place where the boulders in the Erme form natural stepping-stones, we cross the river, and find ourselves at the foot of a small combe, but through which no stream runs, except, as Sampson says, in winter, when the water from the peaty hillside forms a little rill that trickles through its centre. But water has been brought to the spot, as we see, by means of a leat, and the tinners have consequently been able to wash the ore near the spot where they found it. This was chiefly on the banks of the Erme itself, and not in the combe, though the latter was deemed a suitable place for its preparation, as the three small buildings we see there amply testify. One of these is at the bottom of the hollow; the other two further up.

We pass down the valley, finding a path between the stone heaps that cover for a great distance the western bank of the Erme. Soon we arrive at the remains of a building which is of more than ordinary interest as standing within a small court, possibly once covered in, so that what we see may perhaps be the ruins of a house, larger than those usually met with, and having double walls. Below it we notice the heaps of stones are piled up in a similar manner to those we saw on the Black Lane Brook. Several other buildings are passed, and Sampson tells us of another on the further side of the stream, which, he says, is built quite close to one of those curious circular huts found in so many places on the Moor. At length, we reach a little feeder of the Erme, and here Sampson turns away from the greater stream, and the tributary becomes our guide for a short distance. He halts by the side of a mound, covered with heather, and we look around us, expecting to see something of the miners' work. But nothing of this is visible. In the sheltered hollow in which we find ourselves we see only the little stream hastening down, with unceasing murmur, to lose itself in the broader flood; the worn boulders partly wrapped in dripping moss; the grass, and the heather. But Sampson bids us advance a few steps up the hollow, and look upon the mound from above it. This we do, and then we see that it is something very different from what we had supposed. On this side there is a low opening, and looking within we find that what we took to be a natural mound is really a carefully-constructed little edifice, covered with soil. The stones of which it is built are small, and the walls converge as they rise, and form a kind of dome. Sampson tells us that erections of a similar character, mostly however in ruins, are to be seen in other parts of the Moor, and when we ask him for what purpose they were designed, looks very mysterious. But he tells us, nevertheless. It is convenient, sometimes, he says, for the tinners to leave the scenes of their work for a season, and a place in which to lay up their tools where they are not likely to be discovered is then of great advantage to them. He shows us how by means of a few lumps of turf the entrance to the little hut, which from its form we liken to a beehive, could be effectually concealed, and the existence of such a secret store-place never be suspected by any who might happen to pass, and that, he goes on to tell us, is a thing of so rare occurrence that it is likely nobody but the moormen visit the place from the time the tinners leave it until they come again. But the little hut is put to another use now, Sampson says, the mysterious look again coming into his face. We ask what that may be, and regarding us curiously he says that he supposes we are aware that strong waters are occasionally hidden away among the hills. We do not know why he so supposes, but we answer that we think we have heard that such is the case. Then he expresses the opinion that he need say nothing further than that this curious little building is sometimes known as the Smugglers' Cave. That is all. But we have one question more. What purpose was the low wall that sweeps out from the side of the entrance to the hut intended to serve? That, he explains, pointing to the stream, was of the nature of a dam; without it there was a possibility of the weak spoiling the strong.

We return to the bank of the Erme where we take leave of our kind guide. We set our faces down the valley towards the old oak wood of Piles, and the deep cleave that fringes the Moor beyond. Sampson German returns to Huntingdon to continue his search of the ore which by his labour he will turn to gold.

11
Vanishing Foundations

The remains of Bleak House

Though the rambler on Dartmoor in search of relics of a former day will probably be attracted chiefly by the earlier remains that exist there, he will also find that there are others of a later date not undeserving of his attention. These consist of the ruined walls of buildings of various kinds, and they are met with in all the more accessible parts of the Moor, sometimes in the valleys and occasionally on the tops of the hills. In many of the sheltered combes an old farmhouse will be found, roofless and deserted, surrounded by small enclosures, the walls of which are broken down. Often their story is unknown; if the stones could but tell it of what blighted hopes might we not learn, of what strivings with Nature, of what defeats. On the North Teign is the old farm of Mandles, where the settler pushed far out towards the fen; on the South Teign, in Assacombe, is Hamlyn's House, the decaying walls neighbouring the foundations of huts built in an age to which the time of the erection of the

55

homestall is as yesterday. Near the East Dart, where it comes down from the recesses of the Moor, is the building called the Sheepfold, the spacious courtyard adjoining the house being enclosed within a high wall, formed of large blocks of granite. Further down the same stream, below Bellaford, is White Slade, better known by its other name of Snail's House, in consequence of a curious story attaching to it; and still further down, and overlooking the deep gorge below Dartmeet, the crumbling walls of East Combe Cottage. Above the West Dart is Brown's House, and the long wall of a newtake that was never completed. Under Rippon Tor are the vestiges of a former wayside hostelry; below Fox Tor, the ruined house of one who some century ago hoped to subdue the Swincombe Valley; at the head of the leafy vale of Dean Burn, the old walls of Lambs Down Farm. Near Cadaford Bridge and on Wigford Down the walls of dwellings and small enclosures tell us of attempts at cultivation, while on Walkhampton common we see the remains of the "howses" referred to by the jurors who surveyed the bounds of the Forest in 1609. On the Wapsworthy Brook are the scanty ruins of old Longbetor, the former home, so tradition tells us, of a certain squire, who here kept a pack of hounds, and hunted around the Tavy and the Walkham. Many more the rambler will meet with, and though they may not always prove of interest, for this depends very much upon their situation, they will hardly fail to arouse some degree of curiosity.

Other buildings mark the sites of enterprises of a different character. On Middle Brook, on Brent Moor, are the remains of one connected with modern mining operations, known as Petre's Pits House, and also as Uncle Ab's House. According to local report horses were stabled in this building, an upper floor being occupied by the man who was in charge of them. One day the captain set off to visit another mine at some distance from the spot, leaving instructions that a horse was to be sent for him in the evening to Hexworthy, which place he expected to reach late in the day. The execution of this order fell upon an old man named Abbot, or, as he was familiarly called by his comrades, Uncle Ab. It happened to be the day of Brent Fair, and as soon as the captain had departed the men ceased work, and made their way to the village, Uncle Ab remaining behind to look after the horses. Some of the men returned early, and desiring that old Abbot should "keep up the fair," as they termed it, had brought with them a quantity of liquor. Uncle Ab indulged in it too freely, and when the time arrived for him to depart with the horse for the captain was in anything but a fit state for such a duty. However, the old man declared that he would go, and his companions, who were hardly less intoxicated than himself, helped him into the saddle. But they put Uncle Ab with his face to the horse's tail, and giving the animal a smart cut, it started off. It did not go very far, however, for finding itself uncontrolled it stopped and began grazing. Just at that moment the captain appeared, having abandoned his intention of going to Hexworthy, and seeing the old man in such a situation, halted in surprise. "What's the matter, Uncle Ab?" he asked. "Can't fine un; can't fine un," returned Ab. "Can't find what?" "Way the hoss's haid. Should ha' bin to Haxary hours agone, but there bant gettin' nowhere wi' a hoss wi' two tails."

On Western Whitaburrow, in the same locality, the foundations of a building may be seen in the midst of the cairn. These mark the site of a house erected more than sixty years ago by the men engaged in cutting peat at Red Lake, at the time the naphtha works at Shipley were in operation. Their homes being too far distant to permit of their going to and from their labour daily, they built the house as a shelter, and remained there during the week. Some years ago I knew several of the men employed at the ties, and, judging from the stories related by them, I should certainly be of opinion that the tenant of the rabbit warren adjoining did not feel much regret when the fate usually attending similar undertakings on Dartmoor overtook the enterprise at Red Lake. Near Shaugh the name of a certain spot indicates the former existence of a building, all remains of which have now disappeared. This is Windmill Hill, on the edge of the common, and not far from the road leading from Beatland Corner to the Plym. Another building that has now almost entirely disappeared is the house at the disused peat works at Walkham Head. A few years ago a part of this was standing, but now nothing but a few traces of it are to be seen. The turf-house that stood near, in which peat for use at Wheal Friendship Mine was stored, is also no longer in existence. The roof was supported by tall granite posts, and these are all that now remain of it. On the side of Amicombe Hill, and close to the Rattle Brook, is a ruin to which the name of Bleak House has been given, and it is probably quite as deserving of this appellation as the more famous building with which Dickens has familiarised us. It is a mere shell now, but it is not so very many years since that it was habitable, and had it stood nearer to the highway would probably have formed a refuge for many a Weary Willie, for it was not only furnished with beds, but the owners also evidently believed in the policy of the open door. It owed its erection to the peat works at the head of the Rattle Brook, and its desertion to the fact that they did not pay.

While on the subject of dwelling-houses mention may be made of the one that was to be seen for a short time on the summit of Gidleigh Tor. Hardly was it completed than the death of the builder, who had designed it for his residence, took place, and it was pulled down and the materials sold. Portions of the walls may still be seen, and close to it a small octagonal building, apparently intended for a pleasure house. Another little building of this latter kind is to be seen on Halshanger Common, near the farm of that name. This usually goes by the name of the Summer House, but is now a ruin.

Examples of another kind of building found on the Moor are to be seen on Cocks' Tor, the fine frontier height that looks down upon the valley of the Tavy and Tavistock; on Limsboro; and at the foot of the hill rising from the marshy flat between the North Teign and the Walla Brook. These are very small erections, and probably served as shelters for shepherds. It also seems likely that the curious little huts, found occasionally in the walls of the circular pounds, were intended for a similar purpose. Examples of these may be seen in the enclosures near the head of the Yealm, and they bear a great resemblance to the little shelters erected by labourers at the present day. I have seen men engaged in cutting stone in tiny huts of this kind, sometimes using a canvas sheet as a covering. The older ones, however, appear to have been more in the nature of what are known as bee-hive huts, and somewhat similar in character to the miners' secret store-place near the Erme, which we have already noticed. One of these shelters near Grippers Pound, on the Avon, is known as the Blackman's Holt. The Blackman, so the story states, is never seen now, but "he used to be." I cannot say when this was, my information on the subject being very scanty. All I have ever been able to gather is that it was "a good bit agone," which is certainly rather vague. It appears that the individual in question used to delight in frightening people who passed near his house after dark. He would spring out upon them suddenly, but was never seen at any other time. This is rather unsatisfactory. If he only came forth when the night was dark it is difficult to see how people should know that he was black, and it is equally puzzling to understand why anybody should ever have gone to such an out-of-the-way place after nightfall. However, be that as it may; if we cannot now see the Blackman we can at all events see where he lived, and that is quite as much as we are able to do when we endeavour to become acquainted wih the hut dwellers of pre-historic times.

In the Rings on Ryders Plain on Brent Moor are the remains of some very curious little buildings, but it seems probable that these are erections of the miners. The Rings is the name given to a large enclosure in which are numerous hut circles, and the buildings in question have been added at a much later date. They are situated at the higher part of the enclosure, and just within the wall, and consist of little rectangular houses with courts attached. A similar arrangement is seen in other ancient pounds in the locality, but it is not general throughout the Moor.

Among the remains of buildings on high places we may mention the fragment on the summit of Brent Hill. This is sometimes spoken of as The Chapel, but it is also said to have been a windmill. But the older inhabitants of the parish used to speak of it as a look-out house, and from descriptions of it which I gathered many years ago from those who remembered, or whose fathers remembered, when much more of the building existed than at present, it would certianly appear that their idea was correct. Close to it are the foundations of another building which I discovered in 1887. A bonfire was lighted on the hill in celebration of her late Majesty's Jubilee, and the surface turf having been burnt, these were laid bare. The Abbot of Buckfast may have had a chapel on Brent Hill, but it is also very probable that there was a house there to shelter those who at certain times watched the distant hills for the beacon fires.

On the Western Beacon are the foundations of some rectangular buildings, and on Staldon Barrow, on the summit of the lofty hill on the Erme above Harford Bridge, is a little erection known as Hilson's House. There are only three sides to it, but the walls are substantially built of stone taken from the cairn. It is said that a rain gauge was formerly kept in this little house, and there is also a story to the effect that the first grandfather's clock seen in the neighbourhood was made here.

Another building, which, however, does not fall within the category of those we have now been noticing, was once to be seen on the Moor. But the storms of centuries and the hand of the despoiler have robbed us of it. We refer to the Chapel of St. Michael of Halstock, of which nothing now remains but some low banks that enable us to trace its foundations, and those of the small enclosure in which it stood. These occupy a site in a field on the verge of Halstock Down, a part of the commons of Okehampton. It is mentioned in the Forest Perambulation of 1240, and the jurors of 1609 also refer to it. The field in which the few faint vestiges of this ancient sanctuary are to be seen bears the name of Chapel Fields.

12

Rejected by the Builder

A rejected crazing mill stone near Merivale

For the same reason that Babylon was built of brick, the houses on Dartmoor and on its borders were built of stone. On the great plain watered by the Euphrates and the Tigris clay and bitumen were abundant; in the hilly region where the rivers of Devon take their rise granite is everywhere found. Man was guided in his choice of material for his buildings as he was in other matters by circumstances; he took that which lay nearest to hand. Thus we find the homes of the Forest men, and of the franklins of the borderland, the manor houses, the cots of the villagers, and the churches, all built of stone from the Moor. Of stone also were fashioned the water troughs, and pounding troughs, and other utensils needed by the farmer, and sockets sunk in granite blocks received the stanchions of the gates, which swung in them almost as readily as though they had been hung on hinges. Some of these objects, in a partly-finished state, are to be seen today in lonely places on the Moor, for, like the ancient Egyptian monoliths and sculptures, they were cut on the spot where the stone suitable for the required purpose was found. They were left where they now lie in consequence probably of some flaw spoiling the cutter's work.

In my rambles over Dartmoor I have met with a number of these objects, either lying on the turf or built into the wall enclosures. Troughs I have frequently found, but many of these there can be no doubt were made for the tinners. Of such a kind are those at Deep Swincombe, already noticed, and on the Red Lake, the West Glaze, and the Brock Hill stream. These are not only situated close to old tin-works, but are always much more shallow than farmyard troughs. An example of the latter kind is, however, probably seen in an approach to Brent Moor known as Diamond Lane. This path, which is very rugged, forms part of an ancient track, long since disused, though local tradition states that there was once considerable traffic over it. Near where it enters on the common is a large stone hollowed out in the manner of a trough, which according to the countrypeople was placed there for passing ponies and cattle to drink from. But that this could not have been the case is shown by the fact that there are no means of supplying it with water; nor would a drinking-trough be necessary at such a spot, for the Avon flows near the bottom of the lane, and there animals could always be conveniently watered. It is clear that the intention was to remove the trough when completed, but that for some reason it was left unfinished. Another of these objects may be seen by the side of the track running from the south-western corner of Halstock Down to Ockment Hill. Over this a more than ordinary amount of labour was expended, the trough being in compartments, but an unlucky stroke of the stonecutter rendered it useless.

Examples of troughs of another kind are also occasionally met with. These were intended to be used as pounding-troughs, and are similar to the ones seen at farms where cider is made. Being very large, they could not be brought to their destination without great difficulty, and they were therefore usually made in two halves. The broken half of one lies near the King Way in the dip between Corn Ridge and the Sourton Tors, and the half of another may be seen in the hamlet of Sampford Spiney. In a deep, circular groove, a stone, resembling a mill-stone in shape and size, travelled round on its edge, a horse generally supplying the motive power. In this groove the apples were placed and crushed by the stone. Built into the wall of an enclosure belonging to Long Ash Farm, near Merivale, is a stone which has something of the appearance of having been cut to form part of one of these troughs, though it is hardly of sufficient thickness for the purpose.

On the verge of the Moor stones circular in shape, and usually about four feet in diameter, are not infrequently found, and it is rather curious that there should have been some speculation as to their intended use when their form and size renders this sufficiently obvious. Most of them are unfinished millstones and pounding-stones, the latter being of the kind used with the troughs just noticed, while it is not improbable that a few were cut for crazing-mill stones. But some observers have not been content to regard them as being anything so prosaic, and have sought to find other uses for them. The suggestion has consequently been made that they were connected with some mysterious rites, and also that they may have been intended to serve as bases for stone-crosses. In the lane leading from Aish, in the parish of South Brent, to Owley, one of these stones may be seen lying in the centre of an open space where the lane is crossed by another. The space is known as Bulhornstone Cross, locally Bulstone Cross, and this name occurring in connection with the stone gave rise to the belief that a cross once surmounted it. But the supposed base is nothing more than a millstone, and was intended to be used at Owley Mill. A flaw was discovered in it, and it was consequently never taken there, but placed in the centre of the cross-roads on a little mound, and soon becoming weathered, was looked upon by those who were unacquainted with its history as an object of some antiquity. I gathered these particulars many years ago from an old man who remembered when the stone was cut.

Another of these stones was once mistaken for the quoit, or capstone, of a dolmen. The cutter went among the hut circles, near the well-known rows on Long Ash Hill above Merivale, for a suitable stone, and having fashioned it according to his plan, there he left it. As it was resting on some granite blocks, it certainly conveyed the notion of a small dolmen, and this a former well-known local antiquary, allowing his zeal to obscure his judgment, took it to be. It was just in the place where it was likely a dolmen might be found, and being weathered somewhat, he was quite ready to believe it to be a couple of thousand years old, or as many more as the next new theory respecting such monuments might demand. The find was regarded as a very valuable one. it was the first dolmen yet discovered with a worked quoit. Similar objects had been found in India having carved supports and a rude capstone, untouched by the workman's tool; but here the very reverse was exhibited, a carefully finished capstone resting on supports that had been left in a natural state. And Dartmoor, of which the antiquary in question was so fond, was to have the honour of furnishing this unique example of a dolmen. Correspondence with a writer on archæological subjects ensued, and notes were prepared for a paper to be read before the members of a certain association. But unfortunately for those who love a joke this was never written. It was discovered that neither the wild Celt, nor the Three Spinsters had set up the supposed dolmen. The matter was talked about in the locality, and a man came forward with some information that rendered the proposed paper unnecessary. "Twudn' no old man cut thacky stone," he said; "I cut 'n."

On Rippon Tor, and quite close to the cairn with which the hill is crowned, is a circular stone which it has been suggested may have been cut as a base for a cross sculptured on a mass of granite nearby. But it is much more likely that it was intended for Bag Tor Mill; it is precisely of the same character as others seen in different parts of the Moor, and which were undoubtedly intended for millstones. On the same hill is another stone of the kind, but rather larger. This is close to an overhanging rock on the great reave that runs in a north-westerly direction from the tor. Other similarly-cut stones may be seen in Dockwell Brake, in the south-east corner of Brent Moor; at Dockwell Gate, and in the wall near Shipley Tor. In Shipley Brake below the tor I have discovered several. It was on this part of the Moor that stones were usually cut for the mills in the neighbourhood of Brent. I have known many men who remembered when this was done here.

Round stones of a smaller kind are also found on the Moor, while the socketted stones in which the gates were formerly hung are very common. One of the former class may be seen built into the wall of Widecombe Churchyard. Some are also to be seen near Chagford, and at Brent. Of the latter examples are found all round the Moor, but are, perhaps, more numerous on its eastern side, where the primitive mode of hanging gates seems to have continued in use to a later period than in other quarters of it. Indeed, in that part gates are still to be seen hung in the old manner. Two large stones are deserving of mention, though neither can boast of any antiquity. One lies by the side of the track leading through the wood to the cottage at Vixen Tor; the other near Trowlesworthy Tor. The stone by the track was intended for the Plymouth Breakwater, and is beautifully cut; it was, however, rendered useless by a flaw. The stone at Trowlesworthy is of red granite. In shape it resembles a huge cylinder, and it is said to have been intended for the base of a monument. To quarry it and cut it was one thing, to convey it over the Moor was another, and so it lies useless on the turf. Robinson Crusoe made a similar mistake when he hollowed out his canoe too far from the water.

In this notice of the remains on Dartmoor that belong to the historic period it has been possible only to point out where the most remarkable are to be found. The rambler over the waste will not fail to come upon many more, and if he loves that which is old the discovery will lend an additional interest to his wanderings. But though the grey stones that carry us back in imagination to a far distant time, and the objects that awaken thoughts of a day nearer to our own, give to the Moor a peculiar attraction, it is to Nature that it owes its real charm. What man has placed there in a bygone age has a story to tell, and it is one to which we listen with delight, but it does not engross our attention. We hear only a whispering; the tor-crowned height and the stream speak to us in a loud voice. The one is an episode, to which we give ear in passing; the other an eternal history. "In comparison to the work of Nature," says the late Mr. W. F. Collier, in speaking of the stone remains on the Moor, "all interest in them vanishes," and yet we have been lately told, as though the statement should satisfy us, that the few objects of antiquity in the vicinity of the site of a projected undertaking on the Moor which will utterly deface it, shall not be damaged. Of the wild beauties of that part of the Moor which this undertaking will destroy nothing is said. Those who love Dartmoor are to be robbed of these, and may console themselves if they can with the knowledge that a few stones will be left untouched; and this from the member of an association whose professed aim is the preservation of the Moor. While altogether opposed to the ideas of Southey, who thought rose bushes and poor-rates better than steam engines and independencies, and who, as Macaulay points out, discovered that the way to compare the effect of manufactures and agriculture was to stand on a hill and look at a cottage and a factory, and see which was the prettier, we do think that some regard should be paid to the natural beauties of a district; but unfortunately there are those who we verily believe would not hesitate to plaster the tors of Dartmoor with advertisements of soap, or patent medicines, or any other saleable commodity, if they thought they could make money by so doing; but money is not the be-all and the end-all of life, and some there are who find pleasure in other things than the pursuit of it. Dartmoor is one of the few places in England where wild Nature is to be seen. It is hard that the gold-seeker should rob it of its charm. Sir J. Crichton Browne, in his recent presidential address at the annual congress of the Sanitary Inspectors' Association, said that there were grounds for believing that the love of Nature, and an appreciation of its salving power, were increasing amongst the working and middle classes, while it was dying out amongst the affluent. That this love should be increasing amongst the classes that form the larger portion of our population is a healthy sign; that it should be decreasing amongst the class who find enjoyment in flying along the country roads at thirty or forty miles an hour, and catching only a glimpse of the objects they pass through dusty goggles, is not to be wondered at. Those who seek their pleasure in Nature will never be disappointed, and nowhere can she be better studied in her wilder mood than on Dartmoor.